SOUL CITY WANDERING

A London Pilgrimage

FRANK MOLLOY

THE CHOIR PRESS

First published in the United Kingdom in 2020 by
The Choir Press

ISBN 978-1-78963-129-6

Front cover image:
Commuters on London Bridge regularly commemorate
TS Eliot's *The Wasteland*, a century after it was written.
(Courtesy: Matthew Van Gessel).

Rear cover image:
Boudicca's statue on Westminster Bridge. Deep below London's surface
lies a layer of red ash roughly 2,000 years old. It is the burnt remains of the
embryonic Roman settlement razed to the ground by the Celtic warrior queen.
The city's social history essentially starts from this point.
Boudicca not only heralds London's end, but also its beginning.
(Copyright: the author).

CONTENTS

PREFACE

The aim of this book is to inspire travellers to engage with their journeys; to encourage interaction with time, place, motion and emotion, thus reconnecting with one's environment.

The main 'pilgrimage' is an easily navigable route across London combining walking and public transport. It links twelve highly evocative places and uses lyrical expression to amplify a sensory perception of the city.

This book is not about 'hidden London'. Most of the locations are well-known. They have been selected because they have a strong 'synergy'. That is, spaces where the interaction of multiple agents or events produces an effect greater than the sum of their individual significance. In a word: soul.

Two further models of this concept are included. Both are London-themed but a little more compact. 'Romancing the British Museum' is an exploration of that institution's influence on poetry, while 'Ghosts of Swinging London' is a jaunt around Soho, focusing on its impact on rock 'n' roll.

Finally, some hints and tips have been added to help you create your own experiences. Enjoy.

Frank Molloy
02/04/2020

Frank Molloy was born in south London. He has an MA in London history (Birkbeck) and is a qualified Blue Badge Guide (MITG), Westminster Guide and City of London Guide. He has lectured at various institutions including the Museum of London and the National Portrait Gallery. As an accredited journalist, he writes on travel and culture.

SOUL CITY
WANDERING

INTRODUCTION

My City

My city: that's the quickening override crossing from the southern side as London's river vistas glide and muscle into view. It stimulates the senses, breaking down defences. An all-consuming web with a sticky residue.

Kaleidoscopic and psychological interaction of its many dispositions set your mind into a spin. Bewitching and addictive, violent and vindictive, coated with seduction to permeate the skin.

Refusing the engagement, or faking cool detachment, are blithe transparent yearnings for a safety net instead. Dismiss with bile or bathos, apathy or pathos: my city has you beaten, my city has you dead.

Follow down the rabbit hole. Take a journey through its soul. Let yourself be lured into its labyrinthine trap. Use the threaded walls to bind the different channels of your mind; plait the traits into a strand to craft a common map.

Lost in Wandering

Psychogeography: a comparatively modern label for a theme this book seeks to embrace. But what does it mean? In short, it is a journey of emotional interaction with your environment, or the act of experiencing your surroundings on a sensory level. Beyond that, it's an ambiguous term.

Merlin Coverley, in *Psychogeography* (2006), contends the reason why the subject is so nebulous and resistant to definition is that it appears to harbour within it such a welter of seemingly unrelated concepts. As it has mutated, the derivatives have allowed engagement via multiple metaphysical dimensions, traits, currents, vortexes, senses and imprints. So, to start, it might be worth defining more expansively, in so far as that is possible, this intriguing field.

In the 1950s, the French writer Guy Debord defined psychogeography as the interpretation of 'specific effects of the geographical environment, whether consciously organized or not, on the emotions and behavior of individuals'. Indeed, some claim the study's origins are rooted in the situationist movement that Debord spearheaded, having been heavily influenced by the geocultural reflections of contemporary novels such as

Jack Kerouac's *On the Road*. However, it could be argued that the movement had simply assigned a label to a concept already well-established in literature. For example, a generation before the beat got its kicks on Route 66, the Welsh journalist Arthur Machen fantasised about, but ultimately procrastinated in, his plans for a quasi-mystical journey through a city in his 1924 book, *The London Adventure, or the Art of Wandering*. A few years earlier, James Joyce had his protagonists randomly (and operatically) mapping Edwardian Dublin in his novel *Ulysses*.

Coverley hails the nineteenth-century literary concept of the flâneur – celebrating the writer as walker. The flâneur is the idler-about-town who provides a commentary on the urban scene, chronicling the mood of a city. An early manifestation appears in 'The Man of the Crowd', a story written for *Burton's Gentleman's Magazine* in 1840 by Edgar Allan Poe. Here, while wandering the streets of London, the narrator finds himself preoccupied with the meanderings of an old man. The flâneur was embraced by the contemporary French literary scene. In an 1863 essay for *Figaro*, the poet Baudelaire described the perfect flâneur as a 'passionate spectator ... who everywhere rejoices in his incognito ... ceaselessly journeying across the great human desert'.

Considered a guru of psychogeography ever since his 1975 work *Lud Heat*, the Welsh writer Iain Sinclair took studies to a new level in his pioneering 2002 book *London Orbital*. He believes the psychogeographic tradition goes back at least to the Romantic era. He notes that in *Confessions of an English Opium Eater* (1821), Thomas De Quincey found himself in the labyrinth of his mind within the labyrinth of the city. Attempting to steer an escape route, he invoked nautical principles, using the night sky in search of a 'north-west passage', and used this as his thread to guide him through the maze of his obsession.

De Quincey was a devotee of William Wordsworth, who himself, just a decade or so earlier, could be found roaming the Lake District in a seemingly aimless cloudlike wandering, hoping to discover an inner peace. Wordsworth's contemporary William Blake may also be considered a standard bearer for such geo-soul-searching. And from a generation before, the eighteenth-century impresario George Alexander Stevens used local characters to map out his version of the city in the Hogarthian *Adventures of a Speculist*, published posthumously in 1788. William Hogarth himself was a keen practitioner of flâneurity, as were his fellow satirists, John Gay, Jonathan Swift and Ned Ward.

We might even go back millennia to find examples of psychogeography in the classics. In *The Art of Love*, Ovid hijacks the authoritarian and moralistic nature of the eternal city's imperial architecture, replacing it with sites for sensuality. He encourages walkers to appropriate buildings, monuments and landmarks for licentious liaisons, listing by name colonnades, porticos, temples, fountains, law courts, theatres and arenas. Roma is thus subverted and inverted to *amor*. In the words of historian Michael Wood: 'In Ovid's pages, the emperor's grand design for the city becomes a kind of erotic memory map.'

London Psychosis

I had often heard of the world's seven wonders in my reading days at school but I found in London alone thousands.

John Clare

London's overbearing nature has had a major effect on the genre. According to Coverley, 'The literary tradition of London writing that acts as a precursor to psychogeography ... tends towards a uniformly dark picture of the city as the site of crime, poverty and death.'

Aside from Coverley and Sinclair, the chief exponents where modern London is concerned were Ian Nairn and Peter Ackroyd. Nairn (1930–1983) was a contributor to the *Architectural Review*. For his critically acclaimed book *Outrage* (1956), he drove the length of England from Southampton to Carlisle, hunting for the individualism of places. Finding a distinct lack of it, he coined the term *Subtopia* for the urban areas he felt had been failed by town planners. A decade later, *Nairn's London* (1966) was published, a highly influential work which presented, in his words, 'a record of what has moved me between Uxbridge and Dagenham'.

Ackroyd, in particular, suffered acutely from his obsession, most evidently in his hugely successful *London: The Biography* (2000). There had been a plethora of 'grand narrative' histories of London in the decade leading up to Ackroyd's seminal work. To list just a few of the bestsellers: Richard Tames's *A Traveller's History of London* (1992) was a concise overview that could appeal to visitors; Roy Porter's *London: A Social History* (1994) showed the late historian in his element on the capital's struggle with housing, exploitation and poverty; Francis Sheppard's

London: A History (1998) argued in defence of London's national importance; while Stephen Inwood's *A History of London* (1998) was perhaps the most comprehensive general history. These works were generally well-received by scholars, but when *The Biography* was published it was often academically dismissed as being loose and inaccurate with the historical facts.

Yet it was Ackroyd who tried to encapsulate every sense of London. Advocating that it is not just a succession of people, buildings and events, but timeless elements too, such as nature. When expounding on those most famous London inhabitants, the pigeon and the 'cock-sparrer' (with scientifically accurate descriptions), he records parts of the London narrative so rarely covered in its historiography.

This is what sets *The Biography* apart. Yes, it has its flaws, even from a psychogeographic aspect, as urban myths are perpetuated and anchor themselves to far-fetched legend: 'It is believed the cries of Jews murdered in the great expulsion of 1290 can still be heard at low tide in Gravesend.' In addition, some of the metaphysical aspects tend to reflect the writer's wistful, romantic persona when dealing with his pet subject.

Nonetheless, Ackroyd plays with seams of continuity that capture the essence of the city. Page after page, chapter after chapter, every aspect of London life is met as if it were part of some great psychoanalysis. Even on a wet Sunday afternoon in the dullest of suburbs, you feel he would find a particular mood.

'The Difference'

In helping to define psychogeography, it might help to understand what it is not. It is not strolling from A to B while studying interesting buildings. It is not turning off a satnav in the hope of discovering something new or unexpected. (The satnav is not anathema here. It is simply a digital map, and maps are relevant to psychogeography.) And it is not deviating from a standard route just for the sake of doing so. Here we might take on board the gist of Robert Frost's 'The Road Not Taken': that choosing the path less worn should not be judged a praiseworthy philosophy, as in congratulating ourselves it becomes a trivial pursuit of self-satisfaction. In other words, attaching too much importance to choosing life's byways can be folly.

Whose Streets?

Coverley claimed that the term *psychogeography*, a trendy urban buzzword of the 2000s, had fallen into disfavour by the 2018 edition of his book – overused to the point of exhaustion. One reason why the bubble appears to have burst may be due to the controlling nature of its adherents. It occurred to me that the study seems to be the exclusive preserve of middle-class left-wing intellectuals, with little better to do than meander aimlessly around a place they are not familiar with and then write about it, claiming it as a form of political subversion. When I attend talks and lectures conducted by such people, I feel the urge to stand up and shout, 'It's not yours; it's ours!'

But then I'm not sure what I mean by *ours*. I am reminded of a demonstration I saw not long ago in Whitehall. The cause is not important; suffice it to say that a neutral observer might have described it as a political confrontation between left and right. I watched as the protagonists moved towards each other, hurling missiles and invective, until they were ultimately separated by two sets of metal barriers and a thin line of police. Then, small groups from either side began chanting the mantra, 'Whose streets? Our streets!' 'Whose streets? Our streets!' At first, they were out of sync, but as their passionate battle cry reached a crescendo, the entire chorus was locked in complete unison: 'WHOSE STREETS? OUR STREETS!' 'WHOSE STREETS? OUR STREETS!'

I was struck by the irony of the moment. Here was a mass of people in the open urban landscape, unified in a hymn and singularly identifying with their environment. Yet, at the same time, they were signalling their deep factional division and hatred for one another. It's like the absurd futility of the so-called 'London postcode wars': gangs fighting over abstract turf designated by alphanumerics imposed by a postal delivery system. It also reminded me of J G Ballard's novel *High-Rise*, where the close-quarter interaction of residents in a block of luxury apartments gradually causes a disintegration of relationships and gives way to violent tribalism.

Thus it's my contention that psychogeography should not be encouraged as part of a group collective, which often creates conflict, but as a personal experience of the individual, perhaps stretching to a likeminded couple. Notwithstanding, it belongs to everybody. So, if you're a middle-class left-wing intellectual and aimless meandering is your bag, keep on keeping on, and may the road rise up to meet you. You claim your city; I claim mine.

BRANCHES OF PSYCHOGEOGRAPHY

1: The Drifters

Debord's situationist group developed the *dérive* or drift tradition of psychogeography. This generally involves spontaneous journeys by groups of three or four people through the urban landscape in an arbitrary dream-like wandering. The objective is that the emotional disorientation of a randomly encountered space may lead to 'situations' which can be projected as an art form (a sort of abstract impressionism) or act as a catalyst to create radical change.

I am not attracted to this model. In the first place, because of my opposition to the group notion as laid out above, and secondly, because it seems to be rather a narcissistic exercise, as if the purpose is for the environment to bear gifts. Waiting for *it* to fall in love with *you*. In addition, the expectation may lead to forced results or contrived conclusions.

2: The Matrix

This branch involves the search for linear connections or structural intention between existing locations, landmarks or architecture. At first glance, this smacks of the oft-derided pseudoscience of ley lines, but the theory can be intriguing. In *Lud Heat*, Iain Sinclair suggested that the mapping of architect Nicholas Hawksmoor's London churches reveals geometric patterns connected to Egyptian mythology. The more Sinclair connected the dots, the more there seemed to be something emotive in it. The general theme is also explored in Merlin Coverley's *Occult London* (2008).

Studies become more credible when you consider that architects – especially those who had a key impact on urban growth – often belonged to 'secret' societies, and such mystic associations are manifest in their work. Aerial photography of Bath, which has changed little architecturally since the eighteenth century, has revealed that by following a certain path around the city you are paying homage to the secret symbolism of Freemasonry: Lansdown Crescent and Sion Hill represent the serpent; the obelisk section of Royal Avenue is the all-seeing eye; The

Crescent, a crescent moon; The Circus, based on the ancient dimensions of Stonehenge, is the sun, and the massive grouping of The Circus, Gay Street and Queen Square, also with obelisk, represents a key.

The hypothesis links to well-known theories on the structural intentions of antiquity, some of which have attracted serious academic research, such as the layout of the Egyptian pyramids, or the citadel of Machu Picchu. The best-known example in England surrounds Stonehenge. Over recent years, teams of archaeologists have revisited the juxtaposition of natural and man-made structures in this Neolithic landscape. This has led to new research on the interaction of the ancients and their environment. The most comprehensive study, a six-year archaeological dig called the Riverside Project, was led by Professor Mike Parker Pearson, the eminent expert in this field. Having attended several of his lectures, I know he would baulk at any association with 'mystic force fields', but, considering its effect on human emotion, Stonehenge is surely one of the most compelling psychogeographic sites in the world.

3: The Wasteland

This strain is a perception of space or non-place, typically unspoken, unrecorded or non-historic, such as wasteland, industrial park or nondescript habitation, where a new sense of being may be created, or where an erased culture may be rediscovered (if you look hard enough). Here, reality bites. It's finding the mood in the very ordinary and humdrum. Gritty without meaning to be bleak. Trash, but not knowingly so. Neither kitsch nor kitchen sink. Imagine something like an abandoned lorry container, obscured by dull twilight, in a muddy layby, daubed with rough graffiti. The rear doors are open, revealing nothing but a bicycle wheel, a discarded anorak, and one shoe, all just out of reach on the floor. However crude or unromantic this scene may appear, there is a story to be extracted from these ghostly belongings.

It is an element of the central theme of Iain Sinclair's previously mentioned work *London Orbital*. This vast undertaking, in which he explored the 'forced' connection of London's hinterland by traipsing all 117 miles of the capital's recently completed outer ring road, suggests that the scale of psychogeography knows no bounds. (Having circumnavigated the remains of the Roman Wall around the City of London in a previous study, Sinclair, it vaguely occurred to me, was approaching psychogeography in ever-increasing circles. Perhaps one day he'll fill in the middle bit with a study of London's North and South Circular roads.)

There is something of a whimsical quality to this wider aspect, particularly in the linking of places previously unconnected. For example, two motorway rest stops, built at locations 30 miles diametrically opposite each other on the M25, form an axis that splits the metropolis perfectly in half. Once anonymous, now synonymous: London's twin guardians of repose on the road to nowhere are the wonderfully prosaic South Mimms and Clacket Lane.

If you want to get deep down and dirty with this version of psychogeography, the outer suburbs of London are a rich hunting ground. The poet John Betjeman was a trailblazer here. Like De Quincy, he followed his own north-west passage via a tube ride from Baker Street to Amersham, romanticising the mundane London suburbs in his 1973 documentary *Metro-Land*.

I probed a similar Betjemanic vein in the south London suburb of Thornton Heath, the place where I grew up. About seven miles due south of St Paul's Cathedral, with an area of roughly one and a half square miles, it sits so anonymously behind the Norwood hills that it is virtually *terra incognita* for most Londoners. My catalyst was Nikolaus Pevsner's introduction to one of his famous architectural surveys. He singled out the area for sharp criticism when describing the expansion of London's suburbia: 'Continuous building did not spread over the county of London boundary until after World War One, except between London and Croydon where Thornton Heath has a desperate kind of mid-nineteenth-century character.'

That was all I needed. Off I set, Shanks's pony along the four ancient lanes that still crisscross the area, invoking memory, old maps, local newspapers and people I met. It took a few days of my spare time, but the experience was rewarding, the mundane normality now enhanced by the ultra-sound of police sirens, reggae music and rhythmically rattling trains; the atmospheric smell of hospitals, urine and curry houses; the sobering sight of grime, gang culture and old-men pubs. And all haunted by the historic ghosts of colliers, hangmen and highwaymen. To most, Thornton Heath may be as dull a suburb as any. But the heightened sense of being I now feel when I pass through is like receiving multiple radio waves while wearing 3D X-ray specs. Unique, layered, and all mine.

Referring back to Stonehenge as a 'non-place' form, English Heritage, the public preservation trust that administers the site, recently completed a vast project to revert the landscape closer to how they perceived Neolithic man would have experienced it, or, as they put it, 'restore its dignity'. They removed the A344 road that ran alongside the site, as well as the slabbed tarmac car park and walkways. They filled in the pebble-dashed access tunnel underneath the road and demolished all the 1960s-built facilities including the bus shelter, toilet block, ticket kiosk and gift shop. I guess it was for the best. But, standing there recently, I imagined a group of archaeologists, centuries hence, digging the whole site up again and puzzling over the buried remains of all this work. In a way, I miss the old Stonehenge experience. Drive straight to the stone circle, park your car, buy your ticket, then see the ancient ghostly monument stuck incongruously in the middle of the modern world. No fuss, no bother. Now, as the liveried shuttle bus drops you off from the distant multi-million-pound visitor centre, you are surrounded by fields of green. For a moment one might lament, 'I remember when all this used to be concrete.'

4: Sense and Sensibility

Relying on a specific sense can also be part of an experience. The writer Will Self, who taught a psychogeography module at Brunel University, remembered that he once had to physically feel his way home along his regular path, as a thick London fog had descended, making navigation by sight impossible. Welcome to the world of the blind: 'Queer idea of Dublin he must have, tapping his way round by the stones.'

I recall those 'pea-soupers' as a boy in south London waiting for the 133 bus to school. The bus stop was just a hundred paces from our front door and could be negotiated easily enough. The trick was judging if a bus was actually coming. The only points of reference were the deep tremblings of the old Routemaster engine and the increasing size of two ghostly orange eyes emerging from the grey blanket beyond (while I hoped that *they* could see *me*!). Once on board, I would literally feel the journey to school by the left and right turns along the way. The driver surely relied a great deal on sensory mapping. How else could he cope in practically zero visibility?

Of course, sensory perception can be highly influenced by the use of psychoactive substances. We have already touched on De Quincey's drug-induced rambles as an attempt to escape the gravity of his predicament, while the spirit of the situationist movement in the 1950s and '60s often relied on the creative imagination sparked by LSD. Conversely, Will Self used the walks involved in his academic work to help wean himself off his heroin habit.

Although I immensely enjoyed my personal safari, I made the mistake, under a situationist sway, of attempting one journey under narcotic influence. My physical senses were greatly enhanced, and for a while the interaction was pleasing, but a sudden portal into childhood and the inherent lost sense of scale left me in a psychotic state. At one point, I was unable to cross roads owing to a hallucinatory hefty increase in kerb depth and speed of traffic. I ended up lying flat on the ground in the local park, looking directly up at the sky so that I would have no sense of dimension. Quite literally a bad trip.

5: Pillars of the Earth

This tradition considers the repetitive patterns of human behaviour over time, including divergent or migratory paths which paint a new dimension on the urban landscape. The problem with this element in the heart of London is that human imprints may be difficult to experience as the residue is weak. Unlike their suburban or country cousins, inner-city residents rarely stay put. Few are born, get married and die in the same place. Even historically, few Londoners lived for long in the same area. Indeed, as the central metropolis emerged from the roots of the original city (1550–1750), Londoners were especially mobile, migratory, and often short-lived.

To counter this, a softer strain of psychogeography has been introduced that explores the mental impact over time of a compact locale or tangible structure on the local populace. This is sometimes referred to as 'persistence of place'. Take the building at 59 Brick Lane, Whitechapel. Whilst reflecting diverse changes, it has remained a spiritual yoke in the East End, being at various times Huguenot chapel, Methodist church, Jewish synagogue and Islamic mosque.

One may find a synergetic counterpoint with the violent East End psyche at the opposite end of Whitechapel. Here, in 1904, local gang member 'Bulldog' Wallace horrifically blinded a rival using the sharp end of his umbrella at the aptly named Blind Beggar pub. This stands 250 yards east of the first 'Jack the Ripper' murder in Durward Street in 1888, and 250 yards north of the deadly Sidney Street shootout in 1911. The pub's notoriety was further amplified when it became the scene of one of the Kray twins' killings in 1966.

In *Lud Heat*, drawing on the work of Debord and De Quincy before him, Sinclair speculated that the geometric energy of such structures might have an effect on dark minds, his example being the Gothic steeple of Hawksmoor's Christ Church Spitalfields as an epicentre of the 'Jack the Ripper' murders.

Although there is a susceptibility to 'drifting' into conspiracy theories and the occult, the persistence-of-place version, for me, is absorbing, enjoyable and rewarding, and is the main inspiration for *Soul City Wandering*.

POINT 1: PICCADILLY CIRCUS

Route: Start at statue of 'Eros' (Anteros), Piccadilly Circus.

Children of the Revolution (The Urchins' Parade)

Love sending forth indiscriminately, yet with purpose, his missile of kindness.

In eighteen hundred and thirty-three,
A great procession we shall see, of poverty.
And there's the Earl of Shaftesbury.
The champion of philanthropy and charity.
He did so much to help the poor.
He tried so hard to make their voices heard.

Chimney sweeps and young shoeblacks,
Guttersnipes and water jacks will breathe again.
Mudlarks, finders, flower girls,
Tumbling boys with leaps and twirls across the Wen.
Foundlings, orphans, waifs and strays,
Ragamuffins, workhouse runaways.

Our greatness and prosperity
And our superiority provided by
Not the navy, not the bank,
But here's the lot we have to thank, the bitter cry:
Three hundred thousand little girls
Who've made the journey down from Lancashire.

Organ grinders everywhere,
Harps and hurdy-gurdy fare, and sing-along.
See the old professors stride
From the workhouse where they died. And later on ...
Everyone will go to see
The famous Punch and Judy show once more.

Somerstown, the Old Nichol,
The Holy Land, the Mint, the Hole, the Wretched Mile,
The Dark Abyss and Seven Dials,
The rookeries of old St Giles and Jacob's Isle.
Ghosts of ghetto children gone
Echo through the years of buried grief.

Piccadilly Circus

As one of London's great meeting points, Piccadilly Circus is the perfect place to start our journey. Strictly speaking, it's not a 'circus' anymore, as a new one-way system allowed the old roundabout to be reclaimed by the pedestrian.

The world's first neon-lit city centre, the Circus marks the dynamic convergence point of four bustling London districts; Mayfair, St James's, Soho and Covent Garden. Day or night, the place is a vibrant vortex of human activity. Indeed, when the Londoner wants to convey a notion of heavy traffic congestion, they will often exclaim, 'It's like Piccadilly Circus round 'ere!'

The winged statue that adorns the landmark's plinth is a monument to the philanthropist Anthony Ashley Cooper, 7th Earl of Shaftesbury (1801–85). Sculpted by Albert Gilbert, it was erected in 1893. It has never really been clear which figure the statue actually depicts; although it is commonly known as Eros, some claim it to be Anteros, the god of selfless love, and others refer to it as the Angel of Christian Charity. Alternatively, as it is portrayed having just fired an arrow, the figure may be a simple rebus: 'shafts bury'.

Cooper was one of the great radical contributors to modern society. Building on the work of reformers such as Robert Owen, Michael Thomas Sadler and Richard Oastler, he ceaselessly crusaded for government acts in all aspects of social and industrial life in nineteenth-century England, including mines, collieries, factories, working hours and climbing boys (chimney sweeps). He was also a leading campaigner for children's refuges (helping Dr Barnardo), ragged schools, cabman's shelters, the protection of animals, the protection of 'lunatics' and the abolition of slavery.

Cooper's unceasing determination was driven by a battle for political reform within Parliament. For a brief impression of the appalling and scandalous mistreatment of children during the Industrial Revolution in England, we need only look at the concessions Cooper worked to secure in the 1833 Factory Act, painfully extracted via parliamentary inquiry and a royal commission: no workers under nine years old; a maximum working week of sixty-nine hours for thirteen-to-eighteen-year-olds; no workers under eighteen to work between the hours of 8.30 pm and 5.30 am. The Act also called for an 'inspectorate of factories', but policing was inadequate, and so the Act was widely evaded. Nevertheless, Cooper persevered, and managed to force through several more reform acts over the next fifty years of his life.

One of Cooper's supporters, the MP William Cobbett (1763–1835), shamed Parliament into silence when he stood up and addressed the Commons while Cooper's bill was being debated:

Hitherto, we have been told that our navy was the glory of the country and that our maritime commerce and extensive manufactures were the mainstays of the realm. We have also been told that the land had its share in our greatness and should be justly considered the pride and glory of England. The bank also has put in its claim to share in this praise and has stated that public credit is due to it; but now, a most surprising discovery has been made, namely, that all our greatness and prosperity, that our superiority over other nations is owing to 300,000 little girls in Lancashire.

Despite his huge achievements in helping a vast swathe of the population, Cooper remains relatively unknown compared to other nineteenth-century social reformers. His philanthropic contemporaries William Wilberforce and William Booth both made it into the 2002 *100 Greatest Britons* BBC poll. Cooper did not.

POINT 2: WESTMINSTER ABBEY

Route: Walk down Lower Regent Street and continue southbound via Waterloo Place, Duke of York's Steps, Horse Guards Road and Storey's Gate to Westminster Abbey.
(Check website beforehand for visiting info.)

A Vast Unfinished Universe

All human things are subject to decay, and, when Fate summons, monarchs must obey.

What can ye boast of this illustrious sepulchre?
A vast unfinished poem of marble, stone and glass?
The ultimate majestic scene with all its crowning grandeur?
Or an improper indulgence of Elgar and Bach?

Recover the calm in this world of tombs,
Down consecrated aisles, vaulted, dark and winding,
Lest the echoes of our footsteps strike the ear
Through shadows lengthening and resounding.

Aye, a serious walk of High Seriousness
In noiseless and pensive reverence,
Measured, as in another world,
In corners of fabled severance:

Why boast of kings, when giants of science
Deign to challenge eternal law?
Knaves banished to the nave.
This ain't honour, this is war!

Let's hear it for Baron Mendip Welbore Ellis,
Last of the ministers for Over There,
Forlorn hope for the funny little mannikin,
Tea and rebellion in the air.

Need a sincere virtue signal?
Tears for fears that make one weak?
Amongst the specious and unmeaning,
Here the marble seems to speak ...

Take pity on the stricken husband,
Fending off the sting of Death.
Reader, if you seek great art,
Dem bones will leave you out of breath.

Praise be to Esther de la Tour de Gouvernet.
Her gravestone will alone enchant:
Daughter, widow, and refugee
Of the revocation of the edict of Nantes.

More bones, and think how many,
Epic queens and mighty kings.
Hallowed, honoured, leading statesmen,
Now just naked moulderings.

A big hand for the soul of Hardy.
Is his heart in the right place?
May we tease him, while we're at it,
That he hoarded Henry's space?

Hats off to old Salopian Parr,
His spirit and senses overdue,
Buried in the town that finally killed him,
Lived to a hundred and fifty-two.

Respect to Mary Eleanor Bowes,
Botanist, poet, sad countess,
Standing up for female fortune,
Lying in her bridal dress.

A quick shout-out to Cloudesley Shovell,
Dandy on a cushion with a seafaring life.
Lived on a *Sapphire*, died for an emerald,
Murdered on a rock by a fisherman's wife.

As we leave our fine society,
This sacred train of dreamers of dreams,
A floating canopy pervades
And softly dims the lucid themes:

Dust of Armageddon on mysterious mosaics.
Dust of Man that dust is, eddies in the troubled air.
Dust of heroes, common dust, royal dust to grace the dust,
Dust of ages, dust to dust, dust of hymn and prayer.

The precious poets of the past pelt you with a peaceful dust,
With ghostly pleas of sanctuary from dusty old remains.
Reanimated falling dust, and sacred atoms of the dust.
Here sleeps more immortal dust than all the world contains.

Gothic melancholic gloom in towers, vaults and atmosphere,
Vanity is thawing in the silent city founded here,
Yet on the western front of the Empire of the Dead
There lies a path of glory ... where even angels fear to tread.

Westminster Abbey

Westminster Abbey is one of the world's greatest churches. Here religion meets royalty. As the coronation church, where monarchs have been crowned since 1066, it has many kings and queens buried within its walls. Indeed, it is something of a national necropolis. There are over 3,300 tombs here, including many famous names from British history, and they are often grouped together in themes known as 'cluster burials.'

Of all the sensor points along the *Soul City Wandering* trail, Westminster Abbey is easily the most obtrusive. Arthur Machen, an early exponent of the theory of psychogeography, noted reservations about utilising such prominent places in his 1924 book, *The London Adventure*: 'I have grave difficulties over Westminster Abbey. Perhaps because the Abbey has been the text for so many discourses because it is one of the great commonplaces of England.'

It is precisely because it is commonplace that I have included the abbey as an example of what may be experienced at such an obvious site. Indeed, as Machen states later in his book, 'the most amazing things are latent in the commonest'.

Recovering the Calm

The generally respectful atmosphere inside the abbey is largely a result of a 1998 initiative introduced by the dean and chapter entitled 'Recovering the Calm'. There is a touch of irony here because, in medieval and early modern times, huge city churches such as this would have been anything but calm. The noise levels in the nave area would have been increased by the lively day-to-day interaction of the local social and business communities that would have taken advantage of such a sizeable covered area and treated it much like a marketplace.

The example of London's St Paul's Cathedral is well documented. Even in medieval times it was a focus of information sharing. Indeed, the nineteenth-century historian Thomas Carlyle described it as the '*Times* newspaper of the Middle Ages'.

As the centuries progressed, the interior became a thoroughfare as locals used its transepts as a shortcut. It soon developed as a place to trade. Indoor market stalls were set up, some using tombs as handy counters. Horses and mules brought goods through while services continued to take place. The aisles were populated by barbers, blacksmiths and booksellers. The first public lottery was held here. The seventeenth-century diarist Samuel Pepys mentions that bowls were played and teeth pulled. There were checks when situations escalated. Signs went up ordering no wrestling and no urinating. Prostitutes who plied their trade at the Great West Door were moved on, and a bishop threatened to excommunicate anyone who played football.

The nave in St Paul's was the networking hub, known as 'Paul's Walk' or 'the Mediterranean'. It became the place to hang around with your friends, to socialise and to gossip, the idling commentators known as 'Paul's Walkers'. Alexander Pope's line 'For fools rush in where angels fear to tread' is a direct reference to this apparent folly.

It seems to me that reverence shown by today's visitors at both the abbey and St Paul's derives less from their purpose as places of worship and more from their function as VIP Valhallas. Anyhow, 'A Vast Unfinished Universe' explores the lesser-known nooks, crannies and oddities within the abbey that pique my curiosity, ending in homage to its most prominent, yet most anonymous occupant, the unknown soldier.

Scientists' Corner

(On the north side of the nave, just before the rood screen.)

Scientists' Corner, it may be noted, occupies a space in the nave, right 'outside' the rood screen: a physical and symbolic barrier that separated the laity from the sacred part of the church. It may be seen as a psychological power play, therefore, that men who challenge God end up so marginalised.

I remember an irreverent scene of preparation before physicist Stephen Hawking's ashes were interred here in 2018. Next to a rickety old wheelbarrow, a large man in a hi-vis vest knelt on the floor, smoothing the insides of a newly excavated hole with a trowelful of cement. However, in the act of leaning forward, he revealed a rather dark and hairy 'builder's bum'. I was strangely reminded of Hawking's theory of black holes emitting radiation, a theme depicted on his memorial stone.

Baron Mendip Welbore Ellis

(No dedicated gravestone. A mention of his resting place is buried in a long inscription on the monument to his nephew Charles Agar, Archbishop of Dublin, on the north wall of the north quire aisle, just inside the blue gates.)

First Baron Mendip Welbore Ellis was the last government minister to represent America under British rule. He strongly protested against Lord North's motion for the repeal of the American tea duty in 1770. The commentator Junius referred to him as a 'little mannikin', while Horace Walpole nicknamed him 'Forlorn Hope.'

Nightingale (Gascoigne) Monument

(St Michael's chapel in the north transept, parallel to the high altar.)

The Nightingale monument tells the tragic story of Elizabeth Gascoigne, Lady Nightingale, who died in 1731 aged twenty-seven. Heavily pregnant, Lady Nightingale was out walking one day with her husband Joseph when she was fatally struck by lightning. In her death throes, she gave birth to a daughter who survived.

Their son Washington commissioned the French sculptor Roubiliac to carve this marble monument in 1761. In the early models, the skeletal leg of Death is glimpsed creeping from the underworld. In the final rendition, Death has fully leapt out and now brandishes a spear, representing the bolt of lightning, which is pointed directly at Elizabeth. Meanwhile, her husband helplessly tries to ward off the inevitable.

The American writer Washington Irving found the sculpture horrific but claimed it was 'among the most renowned achievements of modern art'. A cursory study of the skeletal details or the folds of cloth on Lady Nightingale's dress makes it hard to disagree.

Lady Elland

(White marble gravestone on the floor of the north ambulatory.)

In the north ambulatory lies the richly inscribed marble gravestone of Lady Elland. The inscription, re-spelt, reads:

Esther de la Tour de Gouvernet, a name renowned in France, and which her excellent endowments of mind and body rendered much more illustrious, was the best of wives and soon the widow of the most noble Lord Elland, eldest son of the Marquis of Halifax. Her extraordinary goodness towards all, her singular dutifulness to her parents made her beloved of all, but by her mother above all. Her soul thus adorned with heavenly graces, she early resigned to heaven and her body to this tomb which her mother, herself almost buried in sorrows as the least mark of her unspeakable grief, made for her. She died the 28th year of her age of the Christian account 1694.

A lower inscription tells us she was the daughter of Huguenot refugees who had fled France in 1685 after the revocation of the Edict of Nantes. This revocation was issued by Louis XIV of France. It denied Huguenots the right to practise their religion, which had been originally been granted to them in 1598.

Thomas Hardy

(Square beige stone on the south transept floor of Poets' Corner.)

Poets' Corner marks the burial place of the illustrious writer and poet Thomas Hardy. After his death, his heart was surgically removed with the intention of it being buried in his garden in his beloved Wessex. A rumour persists that his cat ate it while it was awaiting burial.

In 1911, Hardy wrote a poem called 'The Coronation'. It is themed around an imagined conversation held by the monarchs who are buried in Westminster Abbey. The main contributor to this afterlife discussion is Henry VIII. The problem with this is that this particular monarch is buried in Windsor Castle.

Thomas Parr

(Small white oblong stone on the south transept floor of Poets' Corner.)

Born in 1483, Shropshireman Thomas Parr was said to have lived to the ripest old age of 152. The inscription on his memorial stone claims he saw the reigns of ten monarchs from Edward IV to Charles I, in which case he outlived the entire Tudor dynasty.

According to various legends, Parr fathered a child when he was over a hundred and married for the last time aged 120. His long life he put down to eating well and drinking beer and sherry. When he died in 1635, according to the diarist John Evelyn, it was not from extreme old age, but owing to the foul stench of the London air.

'Old Parr' is mentioned in Dickens's *Dombey and Son* and *The Old Curiosity Shop*, Bram Stoker's *Dracula*, James Joyce's *Finnegans Wake* and the Robert Graves poem 'A Country Mansion'. He also had his portrait painted by the Dutch painter Rubens.

Mary Eleanor Bowes, Countess of Strathmore

(Well-worn black gravestone on the south transept floor of Poets' Corner. Immediately to the left of the memorial stone to Thomas Parr.)

Mary Eleanor Bowes, Countess Dowager of Strathmore, was once the wealthiest heiress in Britain. Referred to as the Unhappy Countess, she was notorious for her licentious lifestyle. After her first husband, John Lyon, 9th Earl of Strathmore, died at sea, Mary married an adventurer called Andrew Stoney. After years of physical and mental abuse from him, she became the first British woman to successfully sue for divorce and keep her property.

A poet and passionate naturalist, Mary corresponded with the great plant collectors of the day, including Joseph Banks and William Paterson. Indeed, she was once described by surgeon Jesse Foot as 'the most intelligent female botanist of the age'.

Mary died in 1800 at the age of fifty-one. She was buried in her diamond-encrusted bridal dress with courtly accessories and a small silver trumpet. She is a direct ancestor of Queen Elizabeth II.

Robert Hauley

(Worn black gravestone on the floor in Poets' Corner. Opposite Dryden's monument.)

This tomb has an indent of a lost brass of a knight in armour. A nineteenth-century inscription notes, 'Robert Hawle, Knight. Murdered in the choir. August 1378.'

A further Latin inscription on the grave, now lost, was recorded in 1600. Roughly translated, it read:

The false anger of the mob and raging swords of soldiers did for me in this renowned refuge of piety, while the priest read mass at the altar. Alas, in my death throes, the faces of the monks were splattered with my blood. The Quire is my witness forever. And now this sanctuary holds me, because it was here that I, the innocent Robert Haule, felt the first sword of death.

In the 1370s, as a result of an English military victory in Castile, Spain, Robert Hauley and his colleague John Shakel held the lucrative ransom rights of the Count of Denia. However, King Richard II and his uncle John of Gaunt, who was trying to claim the Castilian crown, demanded the hostage be handed over to them. Hauley and Shakel refused and were imprisoned in the Tower.

A year later, they escaped and made a plea for sanctuary at Westminster Abbey. In medieval times fugitives could evade their pursuers by seeking refuge in certain sacred buildings. By law they were immune to arrest and entitled to the protection of the church for a period of time. The abbey's western precinct is still recorded on a street sign as 'The Sanctuary.'

The abbot refused to give up Hauley and Shakel. So, in order to capture them, fifty armed men led by the constable of the Tower of London forced their way into the abbey during a mass. Shakel surrendered, but Hauley resisted, and the soldiers surrounded him at the altar and cut him down with swords, also killing a monk in the process. As a result of this shocking incident, the constable was excommunicated and the abbey had to be reconsecrated.

Cloudesley Shovell

(Monument on south quire aisle wall, to right of south-eastern door to cloisters.)

Admiral Sir Cloudesley Shovell was an English naval commander who once captained the ship HMS *Sapphire*. In 1707, the fleet that he commanded was wrecked off the Scilly Isles with the loss of nearly 1,500 souls. The disaster was probably precipitated by the fact that the navigational tables he was using were full of errors. The admiral was washed up alive but, according to legend, was killed by a local woman who was after the emerald ring on his finger.

Shovell's monument was sculpted by Grinling Gibbons in 1708. The *Westmonasterium* is an early eighteenth-century study of the abbey's tombs and monuments by the Reverend John Dart. In it, Dart criticised the memorial to Shovell, saying it reminded him of a 'figure of a Beau, reposing himself against velvet cushions'.

Not far from the abbey, another image of Shovell can be found in a pub sign at Charing Cross. Some time ago, the Ship, which dates back to 1730, merged with the pub opposite named after the admiral. Now, the Ship & Shovell sits uniquely split over two sides of Craven Passage. It is said to have been Benjamin Franklin's local.

As a place for reposing officers, the Royal Navy is well served by the abbey. The Navy's most famous hero, Lord Nelson, understood its impact on the psyche of his men when he rallied them with the battle cry, 'Westminster Abbey or victory.' Despite this, Nelson was buried in St Paul's Cathedral.

In the same year that Nelson was laid to rest, 1806, a life-size wax effigy of him was installed in the abbey as a counterattraction. Dressed in his genuine uniform, it's the only wax effigy in the abbey of someone who is not actually buried there.

Cosmati Pavement

(On the floor of the main altar.)

A mysterious mosaic interset with ancient precious stones. In 1258, the abbot of Westminster returned from a trip to Rome with a family of Italian craftsmen named Cosmati. He commissioned them to design and create this pavement.

At the time it was being laid, there was an ecclesiastical crisis. As a result of the Crusades to the Holy Land, there had been a rediscovery of the work of the ancient Greek philosopher Aristotle. He had once taught that everything relates to a 'first cause' or prime mover (an early 'Big Bang' theory?). Some medieval minds believed Aristotle made more sense than Christian doctrine. The thirteenth-century philosopher Thomas Aquinas argued that the prime mover was God, thus assimilating Aristotelian thought with Christian beliefs.

It is claimed the Cosmati mosaic depicts the known universe of the thirteenth century. It is also said to predict the end of the world, according to a formula in its inscription, after 19,683 years. A very similar floor design features in Holbein's compelling *Ambassadors* portrait in the National Gallery.

Unknown Soldier

(Tomb on the floor at the western end of the church, just inside the entrance.)

The body of the unknown soldier was interred here on Armistice Day, 11 November, in 1920. It represents all soldiers missing in action, presumed dead.

After World War I had ended, a padre on the Western Front discovered a burial place in the yard of a French house dedicated to 'an unknown warrior'. He took the idea to the dean of Westminster Abbey. An unidentified Allied soldier who had been killed during World War I was chosen at random from a number of bodies by a general who had been blinded in action. The body was placed in an English oak coffin and shipped back to Britain in a Royal Navy battleship.

The soldier was given a full state funeral – the only (presumed) commoner to get one. A team of horses that had survived the war together pulled the funeral carriage. The guard of honour was a hundred men who had been awarded the Victoria Cross and a hundred women whose husbands had been listed as missing in action. A quarter of a million people filed past the coffin before it was set in the tomb – the last body buried in the abbey.

The soldier lies with a medieval sword from the royal collection. The coffin is entombed in French soil and covered by a slab of Belgian marble. The brass inscription, made from recast ammunition shells, states that the soldier is British, although he could be of any nationality then allied to the British forces. The tomb is surrounded by poppies – the hardy flower that grew amongst the mud and blood on the Western Front.

The Medal of Honor was awarded to the unknown soldier on behalf of the USA in 1921. In 1923, the Queen Mother placed a wedding bouquet on the tomb. She lost a brother during World War I. Brides at Westminster Abbey have placed their bouquets on the tomb ever since.

POINT 3: HUNGERFORD BRIDGE, EMBANKMENT

Route: Cross Parliament Square towards Westminster Bridge. Walk along Victoria Embankment (or take tube from Westminster to Embankment; exit via south entrance). Climb the riverside stairs up to Hungerford Bridge.

What I Did (Obsessive Killing Disorder)

London, spend the night with me.
Craving over water,
Lure with bondage and escape
The gaze of luminary artists.

London, spend the night with me.
Craving over water,
Dredge up the worst types:
Psychotic, degraded, people on the edge.

London, spend the night with me.
Craving over water,
Invite to the gala
Tramps, druggies, people on the street.

London, spend the night with me.
Craving over water,
Summon the famished ghosts
That loiter on the Thames embankment.

What I did, that spring evening:
Hurled a hobo to his death
On my sadistic spree
(A wolf-man fantasy).

What I did, that summer evening:
Drowned the voice of an angel
In a pool of her own blood,
Strolled around for a couple of hours.

What I did, that autumn evening:
Murdered a civil servant for holding hands,
Stamped on his face with all my might,
Laughed and danced and put on make-up.

What I did, that winter evening:
Butchered the wife for breaking my pipe,
Watched her head sink to the depths,
Made plans for a Sunday roast.

What I did, that spring evening:
Garrotted an impresario for chatting me up,
Forced a flick knife into his throat,
Jumped into a taxi home.

What I did, that summer evening:
Slayed a student who begged for help,
Threw him in the river for fun,
Joked and sang and exchanged kisses.

What I did, that autumn evening:
Killed a bartender for being there,
Kicked him so hard and punctured his spleen,
Captured the moment on film for posterity.

What I did, that winter evening:
Hurled a hobo to his death,
On my sadistic spree
(A Frankenstein fantasy).

Cold inhumanity, burning insanity,
A cold rage seizes one so deep,
So many undone by unthoughtful death.
Dear God! Your very providence seems asleep.

Hungerford Bridge

Over the centuries, London's bridges have been celebrated in art, poetry and song. In recent times, however, a darker side has pervaded. In the years leading up to the time of writing, four Thames crossings have been associated with either politically or religiously motivated murder. In 1978, Waterloo Bridge witnessed the assassination of the Bulgarian dissident writer Georgi Markov by a secret serviceman using a poison-tipped umbrella. In 1982, the Vatican's finance manager Roberto Calvi, known as 'God's banker', was found hanging under Blackfriars Bridge in a suspected Mafia hit. Westminster Bridge and London Bridge have both witnessed horrific scenes in recent years when Islamist terrorists have used them to kill indiscriminately. But perhaps it is Hungerford Bridge, crossing from Lambeth to Charing Cross, that has most reflected the darker countenance of man, having been connected to an extraordinary number of brutal civilian murders, as explored in 'What I Did'.

Hungerford Bridge takes its name from the baronial Hungerford family who in the early fifteenth century took up a residence on the north bank of the Thames. Originating in the town of Hungerford in Berkshire, the family's history is littered with tales of treachery, brutality and murder. The town itself made world headlines in 1987 when a twenty-seven-year-old local man, Michael Ryan, armed with several guns, shot and killed sixteen people, including his mother, and wounded fifteen others, before fatally shooting himself. It is regarded as the first UK civil massacre.

In 1669, the Hungerford family's Thames-side residence burnt down. Twelve years later, a market was established on the site. In 1824, Charles Dickens was sent to work in a factory built here, after his family had fallen on hard times.

The area was cleared in the 1840s to make way for a footbridge which was completed in 1845 by the engineer Isambard Kingdom Brunel. It was the first pedestrian suspension bridge to cross the Thames. In 1864, it was replaced by John Hawkshaw's railway crossing into Charing Cross station. The chains from Brunel's old bridge were reused in his famous Clifton Suspension Bridge. The original brick pile buttresses remain in use.

Public pressure forced the railway company to reincorporate pedestrian walkways on either side of the tracks. The Hungerford foot crossings were given permanence in 2002 when they were reconstructed and renamed the Golden Jubilee pedestrian bridges.

Hungerford Bridge was captured several times on canvas by some of the greatest artists of the impressionist era, including Pissarro, Sisley and Whistler, as well as by Monet in a famous series of paintings while he was staying at the nearby Savoy Hotel.

On the night of 18 April 1986, Michael Lupo left a bar in London and came across an elderly tramp on Hungerford Bridge. Lupo, who had worked at various hair salons and fashion boutiques in cities around the world, was a serial killer. Going by the name of the Wolf Man, he had dedicated his life to sadomasochism and boasted of having had 4,000 lovers. In a sudden rage, Lupo assaulted the tramp, kicked him in the groin and strangled him on the spot. Then he tossed his body over the bridge and into the Thames. A year later, Lupo was given life sentences for four murders. Other suspected murders by him remain unproved.

On 2 June 2008, a twenty-one-year-old man, gripped by jealousy and possessiveness, stabbed fifteen-year-old choirgirl Arsema Dawit more than thirty times in the neck in a frenzied attack at a block of flats near Waterloo station. He left the victim in a lift, lying in a pool of her own blood, with the knife stuck in her lifeless body. Two hours later, the bloodstained killer walked calmly onto Hungerford Bridge, where he dialled the police on his phone and confessed to the murder. For thirty-five minutes the operator kept him talking on the bridge as he threatened to jump into the river. He was finally arrested and later committed to psychiatric care.

On 25 September 2009, a teenage gang laughed and danced on Hungerford Bridge moments after they had fatally attacked a sixty-two-year-old man. The gang, comprising a male and two females, launched the assault on Ian Baynham in Trafalgar Square for holding hands with another man. The subsequent trial heard that the seventeen-year-old girl first kicked Baynham in the groin before he was punched to the ground. The girl then grinned as she repeatedly stamped on the victim's face 'with all her might'. Leaving the man to die on the pavement, the gang made the five-minute walk down to Hungerford Bridge. Here, the girls calmly applied make-up in the lift before emerging to dance on the bridge.

On 13 January 1985, thirty-seven-year-old Nicholas Boyce strangled his thirty-two-year-old wife Christabel after she had apparently provoked him by casting slurs on his manhood and breaking his tobacco pipes. He chopped up her body, filleted the flesh from her bones, cooked it, then wrapped it in newspaper so that it would 'look like someone's Sunday lunch'. He placed her head in a plastic bag but wasn't able to bring himself to remove her contact lenses. He distributed the parcels in rubbish bins around London. Then, holding his three-year-old son's hand, he walked onto Hungerford Bridge and threw his wife's severed head into the river. Sentencing the man to six years, the judge incredibly remarked, 'A man of reasonable self-control might have been similarly provoked ... Before these dreadful events, you were hard-working, and of good character. You were simply unable to get on with your wife.' Ten years previously, the victim had been a governess to Lord Lucan's children, taking turns to look after them with another governess, Sandra Rivett, who was subsequently found battered to death at Lucan's London home.

Edwin Thornley was a London theatre producer and manager of the musician Tommy Steele. On the evening of 14 May 1974, he met a man in Piccadilly and suggested they go for a late drink. After setting off they were followed by two other men. As they crossed Hungerford Bridge, the three men together attacked and robbed Thornley before one of them cut his throat with a flick-knife. They left Thornley dying on the bridge and ran off towards Waterloo station, where they jumped into a taxi home. The official Scotland Yard police artist at this time was John Worsley, famous as the man who made dummy prisoners for a daring escape from a German World War II camp. Instead of issuing the usual photofits, he made incredibly realistic portraits of the suspects which successfully led to their arrest.

On 18 June 1999, at four o'clock in the morning, a gang of six youths viciously attacked two students on Hungerford Bridge, then threw them over the railings into the river. The students were initially accosted by three youths, two males and a female, who had approached them on the bridge from the south side. The students turned and appealed for help from another three youths coming from the north side, but, to their horror, these were friends of the first three and, instead of helping, joined the attack. The students were beaten and kicked unconscious, then thrown into the river after one member of the gang suggested it would be 'fun'. The gang, all with either itinerant or displaced backgrounds, split up and went off in separate directions. One set was later caught on security cameras joking, singing and exchanging kisses; the other set went on to attack another man. One of the students was later rescued after drifting on the tide, but the dead body of twenty-four-year-old Timothy Baxter washed up on the riverbank two days later. The attack was later described in court as senseless, heartless and gratuitous. The grief of Timothy's mother was reflected in her collection of poetry and prose entitled *Losing Timo*.

In the early hours of 30 October 2004, a gang of six teenagers set out to prowl the South Bank in London with the specific intention to 'beat up tramps, druggies or just people on the street'. The worst of these savage attacks on innocent victims occurred at 3 am when the group set upon thirty-seven-year-old David Morley and his friend, who were sitting on a bench at the south stairwell to Hungerford Bridge. Morley was a bar manager who had previously been injured in the Admiral Duncan pub bombing in Soho in 1999. Testimony stated a fourteen-year-old female member of the group repeatedly kicked Morley so hard in the head that it jerked from side to side 'like a football'. She then filmed the rest of the ferocious attack on her mobile phone, saying they were 'making a documentary'. Morley suffered forty injuries, including broken ribs which punctured his spleen, and he bled to death.

Patrick David Mackay, known as the Devil's Disciple, had been imprisoned in various institutions since childhood for a series of antisocial crimes including cruelty to animals, arson and burglary. At the age of fifteen, he was sent to a high-security unit for violent assault and identified as a 'schizoid psychopathic killer'. Described as a dangerous misfit, he built models of Frankenstein's monsters as a 'hobby'. He identified with Adolf Hitler and saw himself as a servant of the Devil. In 1972, at the age of nineteen, he was released from psychiatric care and carried on a life of violent crime. In late January 1974, aged twenty-one, he threw an ageing vagrant to his death from Hungerford Bridge for no apparent reason. Over the following months, he went on a killing spree, brutally murdering four elderly women, kicking to death a shopkeeper, and hacking to death a Catholic priest with an axe. In November 1975, he confessed to several murders and was sentenced to life imprisonment.

POINT 4: REDCROSS WAY, SOUTHWARK

Route: Take the stairs adjacent to Hungerford Bridge up to Charing Cross railway station. Take any of the regular trains to London Bridge. Exit and walk down to Borough High Street. Turn left and walk southbound. Turn right onto Southwark Street and left onto Redcross Way. The Crossbones graveyard tribute is on the left near the junction with Union Street.

Big Daves Gusset

'Where are we now? What place is this? Are we just passing through?'
'I'm not quite sure; all I know is we're well past Waterloo.'
Near the ancient market where the train stopped overhead
Sat a strip of wasteland and stood a burnt-out shed.
Through the window darkly, beneath a wintry pall,
A blade of light illuminated writing on the wall:
BIG DAVES GUSSET, thus permitting me
A literary title possessing no apostrophe.

Undisturbed, and underneath this branded territory,
The shovelled souls of Southwark's stews were sleeping silently.
No garden of remembrance for the outcast dead;
Instead, a quilt of rustling leaves lay on their concrete bed.
Excluded by forgotten suns that gave them up and sank.
Unglistened by the silver thread that glided past their bank.
The only fit memorial, then, for passers-by to ponder:
The size of Dave, his netherwear, and why it caused such wonder.

Redcross Way

My first full-time job was working in a storehouse in Borough, the district immediately south of London Bridge. Back then, in the 1980s, it was still home to London's more noisome industries: in particular, brewing and printing. The ghosts of the industrial past are still there, now mingling with the tourists who bring much-needed money into what is still one of London's poorest areas.

Between 1991 and 1998, as tunnel work progressed on the London Underground Jubilee line extension, the Museum of London Archaeology Service conducted excavations on wasteland close to the historic Borough market. They uncovered an ancient mass burial ground with 'bodies piled on top of one another'. This gruesome find turned out to be a graveyard for the sex workers of London's past, who, as 'punishment' for their profession, had been barred from burial in churchyards or consecrated ground.

The upper layer contained around 150 graves dated between 1800 and 1853. The adults were mostly women aged thirty-five or older. This layer was estimated to be just 1% of the total number of burials here. In other words, the site may have held over 15,000 lost souls dating back to early medieval times.

Today a volunteer group, the Crossbones organisation, campaigns to save the burial plot from development.

On the same stretch of wasteland, graffitied onto the remains of a half-demolished warehouse was the title of this verse, *Big Daves Gusset*. Pure bathos. I took the photograph from a train on the railway bridge above as it funnelled into London Bridge station.

POINT 5: CITY THAMESLINK STATION, NEWGATE STREET

Route: Return to London Bridge station and take any of the regular trains to City Thameslink station; get on at the front of the train. Exit via the north entrance and step out onto Newgate Street opposite St Sepulchre church.

It Tolls for Thee

'Tis Saint Sepulchre's bell. It tolls alas for human guilt.

Sunday: tavern, solo drunken,
More's the reason, more's the pity.
Evening: cavern, so low sunken,
Pondering slices of the City:

What a strange place for a station,
West, the hidden Styx of Wen;
Between, the fall of civilisation;
East, the stony hold of men.

Headlines from the house of doom:
Captain John saved by the Belle.
Body snatched from holy tomb.
Outlook: an unsettled spell.

Relentless escalator daily.
Don't need a ticket to get on board.
You're going to die, say the bells of Old Bailey.
Great Tom tolls for thee, m'Lud.

Hey! You suits on Monday morning,
Macintosh will take his toll.
Don't ignore the prophet's warning:
Profit versus loss of soul.

The tunnel is my secret shadow.
Jesus Christ! I need a piss.
Solitude, before an echo
Joins me from the black abyss.

What's that rushing sound, mine host?
A rapid driving rainstorm, pray?
Will it drown the Holy Ghost?
Will water wash my sins away?

Two hundred tons of metal chunder,
Thrown up from the bowels of hell.
Spewing noise like clapping thunder.
Nick and I ain't feeling well.

As the streaky serpent surges
Close towards me, I can see
The driver's face as it emerges:
A demon laughing maniacally.

Haunted by hallucination,
Hurls the master of my fate
To my final destination,
Croydon, thirteen minutes late.

City Thameslink Station

Snow Hill tunnel carries a railway line under the northern edge of the City of London. It was completed in 1865 during the rebuilding of Smithfield meat market. Snow Hill station operated in the tunnel from 1874 to 1916 before the line was eventually abandoned.

In 1986, the tunnel was restructured to run south from Farringdon Station for about a third of a mile, burrowing under Smithfield, Newgate Street and Ludgate Hill. The line emerges near the River Thames to climb one of the UK's steepest railway inclines to Blackfriars station.

In 1990, a new station opened in the tunnel. It was eventually named 'City' Thameslink in reference to London's financial district. It had entrances at two sites that were once principal access points in the old city wall, Newgate and Ludgate. Between them, under the surface, lay the longest underground railway platform in London.

After last bells were called in one of the few pubs open on a Sunday in the Square Mile, I staggered down the escalators of the station to catch a train home. Alone. The sole pilgrim waiting in the underworld: 'It Tolls for Thee'.

Hidden Styx

Running parallel to the west side of the station, the River Fleet flows underground on its journey towards the Thames. On its east bank, before it was closed in the mid-nineteenth century, stood the infamous Fleet prison.

Stony Hold

Parallel to the east side of the station loomed another notorious prison, Newgate. Hidden below it was a hellhole, a dank, dark dungeon known as the 'Stony Hold' or 'Limbo'. Many visitors to Newgate would have alighted at the original Snow Hill station. The prison was demolished and replaced by the extension of the Old Bailey criminal court in 1904.

Headlines

Next door to the Fleet prison, the first daily English newspaper, the *Daily Courant*, was created in 1702. It was published in a building facing the entrance to Fleet Street, which would become the spiritual home of London's newspaper industry.

Doom

Opposite the station's north entrance stands the church of St Sepulchre-without-Newgate. Founded in 1137, it is the largest parish church in the City of London. In the seventeenth century, the church was linked by an underground tunnel to Newgate prison opposite. On the night before an execution, the sexton would walk through the tunnel and ring the 'Bell of Doom' outside the condemned prisoner's cell to signal imminent death and implore repentance. The bell is still in the church.

Belle

The explorer Captain John Smith was buried in the church of St Sepulchre in 1631. He was the leader of the Jamestown colonists, the first permanent English settlers in America. While there, he was condemned to death by the chief of a Native American tribe but famously saved from execution by the intervention of Princess Pocahontas.

When the celebrated Pocahontas and her retinue visited England in 1616, where else could the Virginia Company lodge them but at the famous Belle Sauvage Inn? This hostelry once stood opposite what is now City Thameslink station's south entrance on Ludgate Hill.

Written records of an inn called Savage's Bell date back to the fifteenth century. William Savage, thought to be the original proprietor, was recorded living locally in Fleet Street. Sir Thomas Wyatt, during his failed rebellion against Bloody Mary in 1554, rested at the inn when he was shut out at Lud Gate. In 1579, it was recorded as one of six inns of London that could be used as a playhouse. Shakespeare may well have been a regular; the Blackfriars Playhouse, a theatre owned by his company, was just yards away. A spooky legend was created during a 1632 performance of Marlowe's *Doctor Faustus* at the Belle Sauvage theatre. It was claimed that the actual Devil himself was conjured up on stage.

In literature, the inn featured in Dickens's *Pickwick Papers* (Sam Weller's father lodged there) and Sir Walter Scott's *Kenilworth*. It has also been depicted many times by artists. As a large coaching inn (an advertisement of 1674 states it had forty guest rooms and stabling for a hundred horses), it remained a busy transport hub for several centuries before a new transport system, the railway, sealed its doom. It was demolished in 1873 to make way for a viaduct, built directly above the current Snow Hill tunnel.

Snatched

The graveyard of St Sepulchre became a notorious haunt for body snatchers, particularly in the early nineteenth century. Such tomb raiders were also known as the 'resurrectionists'. One wonders if they were aware the church was named after the holy tomb in Jerusalem, the site of Christ's resurrection.

Unsettled

The four weathercocks on the church tower have a habit of giving four different opinions on wind direction.

Relentless

The escalators at City Thameslink station are on a high-speed setting – the fastest in London; the City commuters don't have time to hang around! Also, for a long time after the station opened, it was the only one in London without ticket barriers: a generous reflection on City commuter honesty.

Old Bailey

The main bells of St Sepulchre are more famously known as 'the bells of Old Bailey', the ones which claim the debt in the nursery rhyme 'Oranges and Lemons'. These would also toll the hour of execution, signalling a debt repaid to the Grim Reaper.

Great Tom

When it initially opened, City Thameslink station was named St Paul's because of its proximity to the great cathedral at the top of Ludgate Hill. However, this was soon changed to avoid confusion with the tube station of the same name. At the cathedral there is another famous bell. It's known as 'Great Tom' and is tolled every hour, and on the death of certain dignitaries, such as the Lord Mayor of London.

M'Lud

Ludgate Hill is believed to take its name from the pagan King Lud. Indeed, some claim London itself is named after this Celtic warlord.

The visible symbol of the City is a dragon, which appears in boundary markers, coats of arms and street signs. No one is sure of the origin of this representation. The dragon is certainly an ancient Celtic emblem, which may link it with Lud. However, in Germanic and Norse literature, dragons were the greedy guardians of gold, which may serve as an unflattering embodiment of the City of London as monetary powerhouse. It may also be noted that the motif of St Margaret, the parish saint of Westminster (representing the rival seat of political and religious power), is a holy figure holding a cross and forcefully emerging from a dragon.

Other guardians, traditionally bound to the City's mythical founding, are the totemic giants Gog and Magog. The Book of Revelation warns that the dragon, as Satan, will be released from his thousand-year imprisonment, and gather together from the lands of Gog and Magog the vast armies of darkness for the great final battle. Ezekiel 39:6 reads, 'I will send a fire on Magog and those that live independently on the isles shall know that I am the Lord.' According to Genesis, Magog and Lud are grandsons of Noah.

The City's symbols may identify it as a pagan institution, yet its citizens have been worshipping at St Paul's for over 1,400 years, negating the 'godless' insinuations aimed at the City.

Macintosh

In October 1986, as the Snowhill Tunnel was being re-bored, another event of earth-shaking magnitude was occurring in the City: the deregulation of the London stock market. Referred to as the Big Bang, it essentially combined brokering and dealing, with trading moving from floor to computer. It led to greater stock volumes, faster transactions, and the meteoric rise of the IT department. It also saw an end to the traditional stockbroker's uniform of pinstriped suit and bowler hat. It is said that the Big Bang immediately created 1,500 millionaires in the City.

'Macintosh' refers to the personal computer *and* the coat. In Oscar Wilde's *Picture of Dorian Gray*, Lord Henry recalls how he heard a street prophet in a macintosh at Speakers' Corner proclaim Christ-like to a crowd, 'What does it profit a man if he gain the whole world and lose his own soul?' In James Joyce's *Ulysses*, a spectral figure in a macintosh appears at a funeral and is pegged as the Grim Reaper by Leopold Bloom. When counting the number of mourners, he remarks, 'The chap in the macintosh is thirteen. Death's number.'

Rainstorm

Just before the trains enter the north end of the station, they pass under Cock Lane, aptly named as the place where the only licensed brothels in the City were located. In 1688, a decade after completing *Pilgrim's Progress*, John Bunyan collapsed and died here during a rainstorm. In the early eighteenth century, contemporary poets Jonathan Swift and John Gay both describe the torrents of water at Snow Hill caused by rainfall.

Holy Ghost

During the 1760s, there were reports of a poltergeist haunting a property in Cock Lane belonging to the parish clerk of St Sepulchre. The clerk's lodger had supposedly murdered his own sister-in-law in the house. The manner of the haunting, although likely to have been a tool for petty revenge – as noted in Charles Mackay's *Extraordinary Popular Delusions and the Madness of Crowds* – was never satisfactorily explained. The American author Washington Irving briefly stayed in Cock Lane while researching for his own ghost stories.

Water

London's first public drinking fountain was installed next to the railings of St Sepulchre in 1859. It is still there.

POINT 6: SMITHFIELD, WEST SMITHFIELD

Route: Walk down Snow Hill to the left of St Sepulchre church. Cock Lane is on your right. Turn right onto Smithfield Street and right onto West Smithfield.

Seat of the Beast

From Haunch-of-Venison Yard to Shoulder-of-Mutton Alley,
Praise the lord of the loin and the leg.
See Hogarth's beef with the burghers of Calais,
In the place where he hobnobs with Bacon and Egg.

Carve your way round the City of Lud,
Past Poultry and in from the east.
Dripping with history, dripping with blood,
We arrive at the seat of the beast.

Where gluttony's blamed for branding the rump
In the heart of the meaty metropolis,
Enormous pink carcasses bummarees hump
In a night at the living necropolis.

War and Peace brokered the games.
Death twisted artfully through.
We gazed in wonder at the flames
Back when the Old was the New.

A fire lit under the poor plates of meat
Of heretics done to a turn.
Here, her Bloodiness, fowl she would eat;
A butcher's to see 'em all burn,

Up north, a New Road eased the congestion.
The natives (named after coquina?)
Downsized the distance to death from digestion,
Preferring the fat to the leaner.

Cross Cow Cross Street and out to the west,
And perhaps you'll pay some regard
To cannibal tales which some will attest
As you pass by Bleeding Heart Yard.

The henpecked husband of Holborn is one,
Or that legendary enterprise:
Turn south where the Hen and the Chicken run,
And clean-shaven punters made pies.

Smithfield

Smithfield is a historic area north-west of the City. Several grim and violent events have taken place in the immediate environs, and in particular it is a place synonymous with blood, guts and death.

In the early medieval period, jousting tournaments were held here, when it was known as Smoothfield. Hence 'Giltspur' Street. In 1305, the Scottish rebel leader William Wallace was hanged, drawn and quartered here after capture. The northern edge became a plague pit for victims of the Black Death in 1348. The surviving Charterhouse monastery was built on the site in memory of those victims, some of whom were recently exhumed during the excavations for the Crossrail tunnel. If King Death ruled London, then surely Smithfield was the location of his throne. The climax of the great Peasants' Revolt also took place here when mob leader Wat Tyler was stabbed to death by the Mayor of London at Smithfield in 1381.

In 1555, John Rogers, Protestant vicar of nearby St Sepulchre, was burnt to death here, the first of over 200 'Protestant martyrs' executed at the site in the reign of Mary I. It is said that 'Bloody Mary' dined on chicken and wine as she watched the executions from a specially built watchtower near the twelfth-century church of St Bartholomew the Great, which has a history of its own. On the subject of execution, the punishment for poisoners in medieval London was to be put into a large cauldron filled with cold water, then slowly boiled alive. This punishment often took place in Smithfield. It took on average two hours to die.

St Bart's hospital, too, has a history of its own. It was founded in 1123, and refounded in the 1540s by Henry VIII after the dissolution of the monasteries; the only statue in London of that infamous monarch stands above the main gate. In 1628, William Harvey published his pioneering theory on blood circulation at St Bart's. He is buried at St Sepulchre across the road. In literature, Sir Arthur Conan Doyle sets up the first meeting of Dr Watson and Sherlock Holmes in the hospital, before they begin their first murder investigation together, *A Study in Scarlet*.

Cockneys – the nickname for native Londoners – traditionally had to be born within the sound of the Bow bells: the bells of St Mary-le-Bow on Cheapside. For many years, the only place where that was practically possible was the maternity unit at St Bart's. Some claim the word *cockney* is derived from *coquina,* the Latin word for kitchen or cookery. Others believe *cockney* derives from the image of the strutting cockerel. Cock Street runs into Smithfield and the Cock tavern once stood in the market. Most words in traditional cockney rhyming slang are based on food, cooking and eating.

The eighteenth-century English painter William Hogarth was as true a cockney as any. He was born in Smithfield and baptised in St Bartholomew the Great. Two vast half-forgotten paintings by Hogarth decorate the Great Hall of neighbouring St Bart's hospital. In 1748, Hogarth was arrested as a spy by local officials in Calais, France, while sketching the old city gate. In revenge, he painted the scathing *Roast Beef of Old England* as a comparison between the two nations. This painting hangs in the Tate Britain.

The corner of Cock Lane and Giltspur Street was once known as Pye Corner. Today it is marked by a statue of a golden boy. It represents the northerly limit of the Great Fire of London in 1666. When a more credible scapegoat could not be found, the fire was blamed on the sin of gluttony. After all, had the fire not started in Pudding Lane and ended on Pye Corner?

Bartholomew Fair was established at Smithfield in 1133. It was a four-day festival held around the saint's day on 25 August. By the sixteenth century it had become London's largest fair. An early seventeenth-century stage play, *Bartholomew Fair* by Ben Jonson, was devoted to the festivities, while eighteenth-century playwright George Alexander Stevens's poem highlights 'frying black-puddings', 'wild beasts all alive', 'fine sausages fried' and a 'nice pig at the fire'. The fair was closed down by the City authorities in 1855 because of disorder.

Dating back to Saxon times, the infamous Newgate prison, already mentioned, sat on Smithfield's southern edge. Ben Jonson himself had been imprisoned there for killing a man. It was rebuilt after being destroyed during the Gordon Riots in 1780, an episode that formed the backdrop to Charles Dickens's *Barnaby Rudge*: 'While Newgate was burning on the previous night, Barnaby and his father, having been passed among the crowd from hand to hand, stood in Smithfield, on the outskirts of the mob, gazing at the flames.' Dickens later had the fearsome Bill Sikes drag the unfortunate Oliver Twist past Newgate, and then described how the gang-master Fagin spent his last night within 'Those dreadful walls'.

For centuries, a horse fair operated at Smithfield. 'Earls, barons, knights and many citizens who are in town, come to see or buy,' wrote

William Fitzstephen in 1174. The horse fair still existed over 400 years later: 'He's gone into Smithfield to buy your worship a horse' (Shakespeare, *Henry IV, Part 2*).

In more modern times, Smithfield was best known for its famous meat market which claimed to be the largest in the world. It was busiest through the early hours with 'pitchers' unloading and 'bummarees' reloading. It maintained its own police force and its own pub licensing hours. A slaughterhouse was first recorded here in the twelfth century and was probably in operation much earlier. Traders drove livestock from all over the country to the market. In 1830 a man was gored to death in a cattle stampede in High Holborn. Animals were slaughtered here right up to the 1850s. The cattle market closed in 1855.

In 1868, the cold meat market opened. Designed by Horace Jones, who also designed Tower Bridge, it featured an underground refrigeration store. In 1945, 115 workers froze to death when they got trapped in the cold store during a World War Two bombing raid.

North, South, East and West

The Great North Road traditionally began at Smithfield and mileages were measured from here. In 1756, London's first bypass, the New Road (now the A40 Marylebone–Euston Road), was built to bypass the growing shopping area of Oxford Street. The New Road marked the northern boundary of London, and today it marks the northern boundary of the London congestion charge.

Haunch-of-Venison Yard and Shoulder-of-Mutton Alley are actual street names in London. In addition, Bread Street, Milk Street, Poultry, Cornhill, Garlick Hill, Fish Street Hill, Oat Lane and Frying Pan Alley are all within a short walking distance to the east of Smithfield.

'The henpecked husband of Holborn' refers to a story in Charles Dickens's *Pickwick Papers*. As they are making their way west from Smithfield to Holborn, Sam Weller points out a meat factory to Mr Pickwick: 'Wery nice pork-shop that 'ere, sir.' However, he then relates the tale of its owner, the inventor of a huge and powerful sausage-making machine, who mysteriously disappears after constant nagging by his wife. A few months after he has gone missing, a customer turns up complaining of finding buttons in his sausages. The wife recognises the buttons as her husband's, and in anguish tells the man her husband must have committed suicide in his own machine. The man promptly flees from the shop.

Bleeding Heart Yard in Holborn features in the Dickens novel *Little Dorrit* as the home of the Plornish family. The gruesome name is wrapped up in the seventeenth-century legend of Lady Elizabeth Hatton, who became the Devil's lover. She made the mistake of being unfaithful to the Prince of Darkness, and he took his brutal revenge. All that was found of her was a beating heart in the middle of the yard, still pumping blood over the cobblestones.

The 'Hen and Chicken' line refers to the legend of Sweeney Todd, also known as the Demon Barber of Fleet Street, which lies to the south-west of Smithfield. According to the tale, Todd would shave his customers in the shop he rented in Hen & Chicken Court, next to St Dunstan's church on Fleet Street. Next, he placed a towel over their face and slit their throat. He then pulled a lever, and the victim fell through a trapdoor into a cellar connected by a tunnel to the church crypt. Todd descended to chop up the body. The head and bones he piled up in a burial vault. The flesh, heart, liver and kidneys he put into a box and took it to his lover and accomplice, a Mrs Lovett, who ran a bakery at nearby Bell Yard. Her meat pies were said to be highly regarded.

The legend spread through word of mouth, with the sensationalist 'penny dreadfuls' reporting Todd's crimes, trial and execution as fact. They claimed Todd was born into an East End slum in 1756, apprenticed to a knife-maker, jailed for petty theft and sentenced to five years in Newgate. It was said he polished off at least 160 victims in a seventeen-year killing frenzy. His dastardly deeds were only discovered when churchgoers complained of the stench. In court, the jury found him guilty based on the evidence of the victims' jewellery found in his shop. He was hanged, aged forty-five.

The legend really came to the fore in the twentieth century with Stephen Sondheim's hit musical *Sweeney Todd*: A 1993 book by Peter Haining claimed the tale had some basis in fact.

As a final literary inspiration, it may be noted that the late poet laureate John Betjeman also lived in Smithfield.

Today, the statue in the centre of West Smithfield Garden represents 'peace'.

POINT 7: ST BARTHOLOMEW'S HOSPITAL, GILTSPUR STREET

Route: Walk southbound along Giltspur Street. St Bartholomew's hospital is on your left. Pye Corner and the graveyard watchtower are on your right.

The Italian Boy

On a moonless winter island, we lurk among the tombstones,
Honeycombing graveyards and hawking to the sawbones.
Plunging down to dig my earth, beneath the watching tower.
Use a noose to yank it loose within the quarter-hour.
Jack will log the evening's haul: four large, one small, a foetus.
We'll hole up in the Fortune, where Bill and Ben will meet us.

'I first became suspicious when they brought him in the college.
I could see that things weren't right with my post-mortem knowledge:
Note the rigid nature. How fresh the body lies.
The head is cut, the swollen lips, and see the bloodshot eyes?
Blood still coming from the mouth? The teeth have been extracted!
Bruised gums and a broken jaw. And that's when I reacted.'

'May walked in the bar room with a silken handkerchief,

And sunk within it I could make out several human teeth.'
'May knocked on my door and asked a guinea for the set,
But one of them was chipped, and so a lesser price was met.'
'Violence had wrenched them loose. Of that I was so sure.
There were also pieces of sockets, gum and jaw.'

'Yes, I remember Carlo. I saw him quite a bit.
He wore a cage round his neck with two white mice in it.'
'Yes, I remember Carlo. I once spoke to the chap.
Blue coat with grey trousers, and he always wore a cap.'
'Yes, I remember Carlo. But, if I could explain,
He lived with me for just six weeks, down on Drury Lane.'

'I saw the boy outside a pub, so cold and woebegone,
I gave him half a penny and told him to move on.'
'Opposite the pub, I live. I saw the young boy's face.
And then I saw him once again, outside Bishop's place.'
'Bishop has three children, with whom I often play.
I saw that they had two white mice on that particular day.'

'They wanted me to fetch a stiff. A guinea they would pay.
A cautionary nudge made me drive my cab away.'
'I saw May at the watering-house put gin in Bishop's tea.
I heard Bishop saying, "Are you going to Burke me?"'
'Two men carried, down our street, a heavy-looking sack.
A cab drew up alongside and they put it in the back.'

'I heard the police were selling souvenirs in Bethnal Green.'
'I saw the bloodstained bradawl lying at the murder scene.'
'Delve and be a gentleman. The work will keep you fit.'
'But then we got to thinking, *Let's cut the middle bit.*'
No remorse could Bishop, May or Williams comprehend.
Bishop said, 'It was the blood that sold us in the end.'

St Bartholomew's Hospital

'The Italian Boy' is based on the accounts and witness testimonies of a body-snatching trial which took place at the Old Bailey in 1831.

Between 1750 and 1830, as the science of human surgery developed in Britain, there was a distinct lack of cadavers available for students to study. Medical schools had been promised fresh bodies from executions.

But this was still not enough, as there were only about twenty executions per year, and there were over 1,500 medical students in London alone. And so body-snatching became a lucrative industry.

Generally, the process followed a set formula. Women or children followed funerals and reported on the whereabouts of fresh coffins. Local sextons and gravediggers were paid for this information too. During moonless nights, a team of two or three operators would dig a narrow shaft with 'quiet' wooden shovels to expose the top third of a coffin. A crowbar was used to lever off the lid. Then a rope was looped around the neck and the body yanked out and shoved into a sack. A typical shallow grave would take about fifteen minutes to dig. Deeper graves could take up to an hour. The shroud was thrown back. Taking a coffin or shroud was property theft, and thus a criminal act, but the body belonged to God.

Churchyards became honeycombed with empty tombs. The poor suffered most after burying their loved ones. The rich could afford deeper graves, lead coffins or private vaults. Watchtowers were erected to look over graveyards, like the example at St Sepulchre church in Smithfield.

Smithfield was the dark heart of the London industry. It was centred around the Fortune of War pub, which was situated behind St Sepulchre church, opposite St Bart's hospital. This was where shady operators made deals with hospital porters. In particular, there was a big trade in body parts. The role played by the Fortune of War in the body-snatching racket is remembered in an inscription under the statue of the golden boy at nearby Pye Corner. It was also depicted in the British television drama *The Frankenstein Chronicles*.

The best 'season' for body-snatching was November to February. This was when anatomy classes were mainly held as the bodies would stay colder for longer. Up to ten bodies a night could be managed by a professional team. Babies were taken too. At £16 per body, and taking around 300 in a good season, one could earn up to £5,000 a year: a 'gentleman's' salary.

Over 200 families made their living from the grisly trade in London, but there were inherent risks. Operators had a chance of catching diseases, such as smallpox, from dead bodies. Some coffins were booby-trapped with explosives. There were frequent lynchings by mobs who saw them as the lowest of the low, and there were gang wars too.

The Borough gang, in particular, were prolific. In one year, they took 505 bodies in all. One gang member kept a diary with the following entries typical:

> *Nov 29, 1811: got 3: Jack, Ben and me 2 in Bethnal Green at 4am, Bill*
> *and Daniel 1 in St Bart's.*
> *Feb 28, 1812: Met at Jacks. Got 4 large, 1 small and a foetus. Got*
> *drunk in Fortune of War.*

But perhaps the most infamous partnership in London was that of Bishop, May and Williams, who also operated from the Fortune of War. Here, they once tricked the Borough gang into digging up rotting bodies. Like Edinburgh's infamous duo Burke and Hare, this trio began to transgress the law, murdering their victims and selling the bodies direct to the surgeons, in effect cutting out the whole labour-intensive 'grave-digging' stage. Bishop, May and Williams would meet their victims in pubs and spike their drinks with laudanum. At a safe house in Bethnal Green, they would drown their victims in a well, then hang them upside down until the laudanum drained from the body, before whisking it off to be sold.

On 5 November 1831, Bishop and May delivered the suspiciously fresh corpse of a fourteen-year-old boy to the King's College School of Anatomy in the Strand. They had previously demanded twelve guineas for the body at Guy's hospital but had been refused. On inspection by the director of anatomy, it was noted that *rigor mortis* had not fully set in, and the gums were still bleeding from where the boy's teeth had been pulled out. The anatomists kept Bishop and May talking while a porter summoned the police. The police identified the body as that of Carlo Ferrari, an Italian street urchin from Piedmont who had made a living showing his pet white mice. The police then opened the crime scene in Bethnal Green to the public, charging five shillings for viewing, and selling practically everything inside as souvenirs.

At the subsequent trial, Bishop, May and Williams were all found guilty of murder. Williams confessed to supplying 1,000 bodies over four years and to sixty murders, although some estimate the gang killed at least a hundred more. Bishop and Williams were hanged, and their bodies handed over to anatomists. May was jailed.

The other scandal exposed by the trial was the custom of children being sent to big cities to act as street musicians or pedlars under a gangmaster, who allegedly supervised the children in exchange for a percentage of their profit. The racket formed the basis of the plot for Charles Dickens's *Oliver Twist* some five years later.

In 1832, the practice of body-snatching effectively ended, as the Anatomy Act entitled surgeons to the plentiful supply of bodies of those who had died in the workhouse.

POINT 8: POSTMAN'S PARK, ALDERSGATE

SARAH·SMITH PANTOMIME ARTISTE
AT PRINCE'S·THEATRE
DIED OF TERRIBLE INJURIES RECEIVED
WHEN ATTEMPTING IN HER INFLAMMABLE DRESS
TO EXTINGUISH THE FLAMES WHICH HAD
ENVELOPED HER COMPANION
JANUARY·24·1863

Route: Turn left onto Newgate Street and walk eastbound. Turn left onto King Edward Street. Postman's Park is further down on the right.

The Truth Is Somewhat More Prosaic

Sarah Smith, in pantomime, at the Prince's Theatre,
Died of the terrible injuries received
Attempting to extinguish the flames on her companion,
Twenty-fourth of January, 1863.

This tribute, dedicated to heroic selfless sacrifice,
Lends itself to poignant poetry.
However, as the actual truth is somewhat more prosaic,
Romantic verse becomes the casualty:

Sarah Gibson, ballet dancer at the Princess Theatre,
Died of the terrible injuries received
In Middlesex hospital, a few days after her dress caught fire
on stage during a live performance, despite the best efforts
of the stage manager, Mr Robert Roxby, and others, who
tried to extinguish the flames,
Twenty-eighth of January, 1863.

Postman's Park

Postman's Park, a small green space in Aldersgate, is made up of three churchyards: St Botolph's Aldersgate, St Leonard's Foster Lane and Christchurch Greyfriars. Its name reflects the one-time proximity of several major buildings that made up the national headquarters of the General Post Office. Indeed, in the early twentieth century, this area was known as the Post Office quarter, and the nearby St Paul's underground station was named 'Post Office' until 1937. Today, all the postal buildings are long gone. Thus *Postman's Park* is something of a misnomer, in that the chances of finding a postman, or postwoman, sitting down to have their lunch here today are negligible.

If one *is* spotted on a prandial outing, perhaps they have been attracted on hearing that a tropical banana tree grows here. However, their appetites will be disappointed, as this variety does not produce any bananas, and even if it did, they would be inedible. Another rare non-indigenous tree planted here is the *Davidia*. It was originally introduced to this country from China by the eminent plant collector Ernest Wilson. The deceiving shapes created by its large white bracts have induced folk to label it with all kinds of names including *handkerchief tree*, *dove tree* and *ghost tree*.

In the centre of Postman's Park sits the Wall of Sacrifice. This is a memorial cloister commemorating heroic sacrifice on behalf of others, conceived of by the nineteenth-century British artist George Frederic Watts. The tributes are inscribed on Royal Doulton tiles. The memorial was initially created for Queen Victoria's Golden Jubilee in 1887 but didn't officially open until three years before Watts's death in 1904. A small wooden statue of him stands in the centre of the cloister. His wife Mary continued to add to the tiles. The most recent was added in 2009.

The oldest memorial on the wall is dedicated to Sarah Smith. However, this was a stage name, and almost all the other facts as stated on the tiles are incorrect. As revealed in the last verse, the truth is somewhat more prosaic.

The Wall of Sacrifice featured in the 2004 movie *Closer* starring Julia Roberts, Jude Law and Natalie Portman. The character played by Portman sees the name Alice Ayres on one of the tributes and adopts it as a false name

Despite all the apparent deceptions, Aldersgate has evoked spiritual moments of truth. It was the site of the evangelical conversion for the founder of Methodism, John Wesley, on 24 May 1738. The date is commemorated in the Methodist Church as Aldersgate Day. Just a few days earlier, his brother Charles had a similar conversion on Little Britain, opposite the churchyard. Their father Samuel was curate of St Botolph's Aldersgate when he married his wife Susanna, known as the Mother of Methodism. A stained-glass window in the church depicts John Wesley preaching in London.

POINT 9: ST FOSTER'S CHURCH, FOSTER LANE

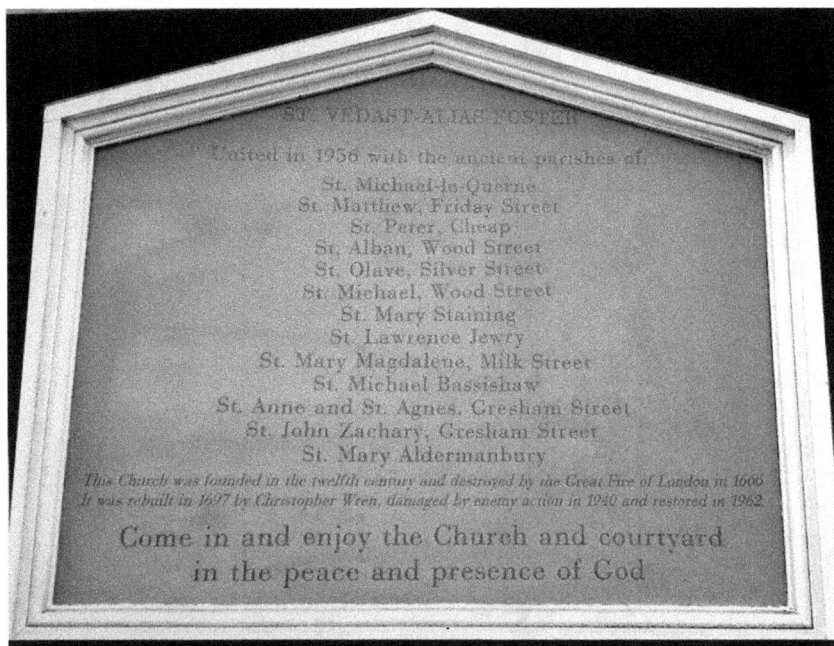

ST VEDAST-ALIAS-FOSTER

United in 1956 with the ancient parishes of:

St. Michael-le-Querne
St. Matthew, Friday Street
St. Peter, Cheap
St. Alban, Wood Street
St. Olave, Silver Street
St. Michael, Wood Street
St. Mary Staining
St. Lawrence Jewry
St. Mary Magdalene, Milk Street
St. Michael Bassishaw
St. Anne and St. Agnes, Gresham Street
St. John Zachary, Gresham Street
St. Mary Aldermanbury

This Church was founded in the twelfth century and destroyed by the Great Fire of London in 1666. It was rebuilt in 1697 by Christopher Wren, damaged by enemy action in 1940 and restored in 1962

Come in and enjoy the Church and courtyard
in the peace and presence of God

Route: Leave Postman's Park by the eastern exit adjacent to St Botolph's Aldersgate Church. Turn right onto Aldersgate Street, left onto Gresham St and right onto Foster Lane. St Vedast-alias-Foster church is further down on the left.

Foster Father

'Bloody 'ell! It's *so* quiet.
It's bloody quiet in 'ere.'
'Yes, son, it's very quiet.
You really shouldn't swear.

'After all, this is a place
Where people come to pray:
A *c-h-blank-blank-c-h*.
What's missing, by the way?

'What *are* you doing? Put that back!
That's Our Lord's thorny crown.
What's your name? Bardolph? Heavens!
If it isn't nailed down!'

'Pardon me for lookin'.
It ain't like *When in Rome.*
"Oh, Father! Please forgive me!"
'Oo's Bardolph when at 'ome?'

'Never mind. Forget it.
Come on, honeybunch.
I think that it's stopped raining.
Let's go and get some lunch.'

'Ah! I got it! Clever!
Dad, *"you are"* on form today.
'Ere ... the pulpit is impressive.
Well, I fink, anyway.'

'Gibbons, I should imagine,
Judging by the carving.'
'Cor! You know yer stuff, don'tcha?
Come on. Let's go. I'm starvin'.'

St Foster's Church

The uniquely named church of St Vedast-alias-Foster stands in the shadow of the mighty dome of St Paul's Cathedral. St Vedast (also known as Vedastus, Vaast, Waast and Gaston) was a sixth-century bishop of northern Gaul and an advisor to the Frankish king Clovis. There is a St Vedast church in Lincolnshire and there was one in Norfolk. But somehow, in London, the name morphed into *Foster*.

The first church on 'Foster Lane' was built in the twelfth century. Remodelled several times in the medieval period, it was badly damaged in the Great Fire of London. It was rebuilt by Sir Christopher Wren in 1673. The spire, thought to be by Christopher Wren's assistant, Nicholas Hawksmoor, was added in 1712.

The church was badly damaged again during the Blitz. After the war, a rebuilding programme was supervised by the newly installed rector Canon

Charles Mortlock. St Foster's initially adopted the parishes of no fewer than thirteen former city churches that had either been destroyed or demolished: St Alban Wood Street, St Anne & St Agnes, St Lawrence Jewry, St Mary Aldermanbury, St Michael-le-Querne, St Matthew Friday Street, St Peter Chepe, St Olave Silver Street, St Michael Wood Street, St Mary Staining, St Mary Magdalene Milk Street, St John Zachary and St Michael Bassishaw. Of these, only three were re-established: St Anne & St Agnes and St Lawrence Jewry in London, and St Mary Aldermanbury in Fulton, Missouri.

St Foster's became a place of refuge for the orphaned furniture of ruined churches including St Anne & St Agnes, St Christopher-le-Stock in Threadneedle Street, and St Bartholomew-by-the-Exchange. It even managed to salvage a section of Roman mosaic flooring discovered when St Matthew Friday Street was torn down in 1884. The exquisite seventeenth-century pulpit came from All Hallows, Bread Street. It was carved by Grinling Gibbons and features his idiosyncratic 'logo', open peapods.

Mortlock is a fascinating character. It was he who was responsible for uniting and accommodating the other parishes. He also ensured St Foster's was reconstructed within its seventeenth-century shell. He was an advocate of the preservation of religious heritage, writing an article for the *Daily Telegraph* in 1947 entitled 'Restoring the City's War Damaged Churches'. He was also a member of the Parochial Church Council, an influential architectural body which included John Betjeman, himself a churchwarden at St Fosters.

A relief in the cloister garden depicts the head of Mortlock. It was carved by the famous sculptor Jacob Epstein in 1936. The two were great friends. Indeed, Mortlock conducted Epstein's memorial at St Paul's Cathedral in 1959.

In his will, Epstein left Mortlock his huge biblical sculpture *Ecce Homo*. The artist could never find a permanent home for it, and Mortlock had similar difficulties. After his death, it was donated to Coventry Cathedral.

Mortlock was also an admirer of the German Jewish painter Hans Feibusch. The mutual respect is manifest in that artist's largest mural in St Alban's church, Holborn, where Mortlock is depicted alongside its incumbent vicar.

Mortlock wrote several books, including *Famous London Churches*

(1934). As a journalist, he contributed pieces to a number of wide-ranging journals including the *Daily Telegraph, Punch* and *Country Life*. He was also a respected drama and ballet critic.

He penned a series of articles for the *Church Times* under the pseudonym 'Urbanus'. Many carried psychogeographic undertones, such as 'A Strange Week', published in the *Church Times* on 1 September 1939, just two days before the outbreak of World War II:

> *To one attuned to the life of a city ... nothing is more characteristic than its customary sounds. The good Londoner waking in the night can generally tell the hour from the noises drifting from without into his bedroom. The murmur of a great city by night is comforting to those who lie abed in its midst.*

A fellow of the Society of Antiquarians, Mortlock was a passionate student of archaeology. As a correspondent, he covered the work of the British Egyptologist Sir Flinders Petrie during his 1920s Palestinian project. In 1935, he accompanied Petrie's former assistant James Leslie Starkey as Starkey made one of the most important discoveries in the history of Biblical archaeology, the Lachish Letters. Written on shards of pottery or *ostraca*, these texts shed light on events described in the Old Testament. Mortlock was there to proudly record the moment.

Mortlock's passion for antiquities enabled St Foster's to forge a fascinating link to the world's bestselling mystery writer, Agatha Christie. Born Agatha Miller in 1890, the daughter of a foster child, she married her first husband Archibald Christie in 1914. Her first novel was published in 1920.

In 1928, after a bitter and public divorce, Christie decided she wanted to travel more extensively. She packed her trunk, said goodbye to the media circus, and off she went on the Orient Express. After staying a while in Istanbul, she moved on to Baghdad, where she was invited to join a party of British archaeologists excavating the site of Ur.

In 1930, she returned to Iraq, where she fell in love with the twenty-six-year-old archaeologist Max Mallowan, almost fourteen years her junior. Within six months they were married. Mallowan was a frequent visitor to Mortlock at St Foster's.

Over the years, Christie often accompanied her husband on archaeological expeditions, making a considerable contribution to their recording and documentation. Her novels were also greatly influenced by her Middle Eastern adventures. They included *They Came to Baghdad, Murder in Mesopotamia*, and perhaps her most famous work, *Murder on the Orient Express*, which was dedicated to her new husband.

During the 1950s, Mallowan, now a field director for the British Museum and the British School of Archaeology in Iraq, led an excavation at the Nimrud palace. It was a well-publicised expedition, thanks to the fact that the *Daily Telegraph*'s special correspondent on the dig was Mortlock.

During the dig, an ancient stone tablet was discovered by Mallowan's team. It had once been part of the wall of a ziggurat in the city of Kalhu (biblical Calah, modern-day Nimrud). Inscribed in cuneiform script, it reads:

Shalmaneser the great, king of Assyria, ruler of the universe, son of Ashurnasirpal the great, king of Assyria, ruler of the universe, son of Tukulti-Ninurta the great, king of Assyria, ruler of the universe. The wall of the ziggurat of Kalhu.

Shalmaneser III reigned between approximately 858 and 824 BC. Much was already known about him thanks to the discovery in 1846 of the 'Black Obelisk'. Now on display at the British Museum, this well-preserved slab of limestone records many of his deeds and conquests. Significantly, it also bears the earliest mention of a biblical character in history: Jehu, king of Israel.

The tablet discovered by Mallowan's team was passed to the Syrian government, who in turn gave it as a gift to Mortlock. Today, it is found on the wall of St Foster's garden cloister near the Roman mosaic. A small number of similarly inscribed stones have been discovered at the Nimrud site, and each should be treasured, as it's doubtful we will learn any more about King Shalmaneser III; the archaeological remains at Nimrud were destroyed by Islamist militants between 2015 and 2016.

POINT 10: WOOD STREET,
JUNCTION WITH CHEAPSIDE

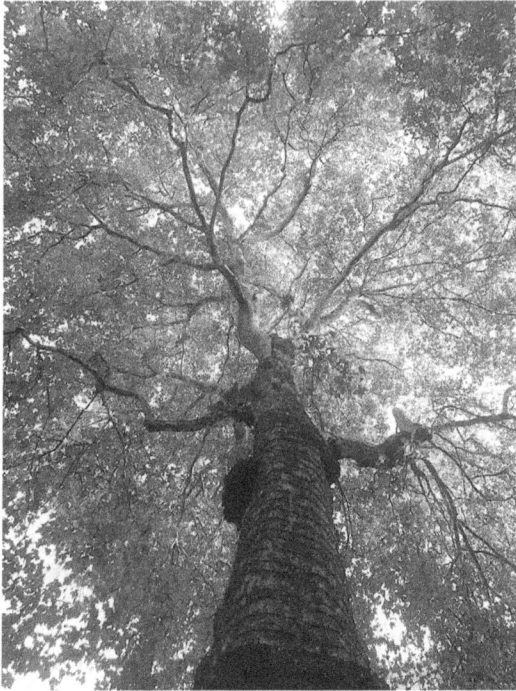

Route: To the left of St Vedast on Foster Lane, follow the alleyway Priest Court to Gutter Lane. Take Goldsmith Street opposite, then turn right onto Wood St and follow to its junction with Cheapside.

Last of the Mohicans *(Mio Platano Amato)*

Because it is a non-native hybrid, there is no mythology and folklore associated with the London plane.

The Woodland Trust

A tree. A visible, living tree.

Intertwining the occident and orient by accident.
Rootless cosmopolitan shackled by its locks.
Soaring eighty feet, yet it's hidden in the shadows.
An interloping rogue amid the steel and concrete blocks.

Surviving by regenerative bark exfoliation.
Resilient chirpy cockney, as native as can be.
Cradling the songbirds that sing of joy and pain.
An old romantic guru of ancient reverie.

Confronting the pollution of stupendous roars of traffic.
Rebel eco-warrior unravelling the vapours.
Protecting local commerce throughout its lone existence.
A refugee and migrant sheltering its neighbours.

Raking its rhizomes through the ravages of time.
Relic of our history (the tree does not forget).
Spreading out its limbs on a city-centre corner.
A rugged Jesse emblem; an old cross surrogate.

Jeremiah, Obadiah, Hannah Canner, Uncle Bill.
Remembered by the reaper of decaying fallen stone.
I hope and pray that rough winds won't shake its resistance.
Against the odds, this real-life superhero holds its own.

Wood Street Plane Tree

The London plane tree is a remarkable specimen of life. It is the result of accidental co-operation between nature and man, and an example of how globalisation can have a positive effect on the environment.

Rootless Cosmopolitan

Over 350 years ago, a chance hybridisation occurred between two trees of the same species that had been brought together from opposite sides of the planet: the Asian (eastern) sycamore and the American (western) sycamore.

British tree experts soon realised that this new hybrid had properties that would allow it to resist the sooty pollution of growing cities. In addition, the fine-grained wood was tough and almost impossible to split. Its hardwearing attributes made it ideal for furniture, flooring, butcher blocks etc. It was also used to make wheels for ox carts.

The tree cannot breed itself, having to be physically planted. The first successful plantings in Britain were in Cambridgeshire between 1660 and

1680; they're still growing. A 1749 specimen planted in Bryanston School, Dorset, has reached a height of 164 feet, making it one of the tallest trees in the UK, while the forty-foot girth of the example at Mottisfont Abbey in Hampshire makes it one of the nation's thickest trees.

The wide planting of this hybrid in the growing industrial capital led it to be named the London plane. It is a tree well-loved by Londoners. In the 2010 guide *The Great Trees of London*, eight out of the ten most popular central London trees were plane trees. In that guide, I championed my personal favourite: a London plane which stands at the junction of Cheapside and Wood Street in the City of London.

Rogue Interloper

Planted at the cost of sixpence about 200 years ago, the Wood Street plane is recognised as the oldest tree in the square mile.

Despite its eighty-foot height, it stands in the shadow of the architectural battle for space that rages in the financial centre. Britain's most prominent designers fight hand-to-hand with an armoury of styles. In Wood Street, we are met by the surviving tower of the seventeenth-century St Alban's church, a Christopher Wren rebuild based on an original Inigo Jones design, now a private residence. To the left, the triangular sections of a glass curved roof are the unmistakable sign of a Norman Foster office building. Next door, the brightly coloured air vents are the inimitable external elements of Foster's 'nemesis' Richard Rogers. On the opposite side is the City of London police HQ. Constructed in 1965 in Italianate style, it was the last completed design by Donald McMorran. Next to this, we have the work of the comparative 'new kid on the block' Eric Parry. Finally, we have 125 London Wall, with Terry Farrell making the most of softly coloured cladding and glass.

Resilient Cockney

Being 'born' on Wood Street, our specimen is a native Londoner. Indeed, it is about as cockney as you can get; the famous Bow bells are within deafening distance across the road.

Romantic Guru

Set equidistant from Temple Bar in the west and Aldgate in the east, the tree's environs form the torso of the world's greatest financial market. Around it beats the heart of banking, flows the lifeblood of insurance, pulsates the nerve centre of trading and investments. It might seem all fairly perfunctory to the average eye, but for those in search of a more artistic soul, there are plenty of literary echoes in the immediate vicinity: John Milton and John Donne were born across the road on Bread Street. Thomas Hood was born on Poultry. John Keats lived above the Queen's Arms pub at 71 Cheapside, where he wrote such classics as 'On First Looking into Chapman's Homer' and 'Ode on a Grecian Urn'. Chaucer, Shakespeare, Austen and Dickens all set scenes here, and it was the main location for Thomas Middleton's 1613 comedy *A Chaste Maid in Cheapside*.

Regarding literary mentions of the tree itself, Leigh Hunt, in *The Town* (1848), tells the story of a local girl who had no knowledge of the tree:

> *A child was shown us who was said never to have beheld a tree but the one in St Paul's Churchyard. Whenever a tree was mentioned, it was this one; she had no conception of any other, not even of the remote tree in Cheapside.*

In his popular history *Old and New London* (1878) the Victorian writer and poet Walter Thornbury described the tree thus:

> *How pleasantly on a summer morning that last of the Mohicans, the green plane-tree, now deserted by the rooks, at the corner of Wood Street, flutters its leaves!*

On the subject of the tree's possible inhabitants, in his botanical studies of London, the naturalist James Mitchell remarked in 1831 that 'a pair of crows have this spring taken up their abode within the city, and built their nest in the top of the lofty plane-tree in Wood-street, close to Cheapside.' A twentieth-century literary classic suggests a different resident: in Hugh Lofting's *Doctor Dolittle* series, 'Cheapside' is the name belonging to the little cockney sparrow.

On a final note here, nearly every book, blog and article that I have read on William Wordsworth's 'The Reverie of Poor Susan' happily trots out the fallacy that the Wood Street plane was specifically referred to. This would indeed add to the tree's miraculous reputation, considering the poem was written in 1797 and the tree planted in 1821. Perhaps there was an earlier tree? Even if there was, Wordsworth does not specifically mention it in the poem which reads, 'At the corner of Wood Street, when daylight appears, / Hangs a thrush that sings loud, it has sung for three years.' It is most likely the thrush was hanging in a cage. Had it been *in* the tree, I suspect Wordsworth would have used the word *sits*, not *hangs*. However, the fact that the nation's most romantic poet chose to use this particular London street corner as a setting certainly adds to the literary mysticism of the place.

Rebel Eco-warrior

For 2,000 years, the thoroughfare of Cheapside has been one of the busiest in London, and the traffic has brought its share of pollution to the district. Before the Great Fire, the seventeenth-century diarist John Evelyn noted the surrounding air 'is poisoned with so thick and dark a fog'. In the eighteenth century, Wordsworth's aforementioned 'Reverie of Poor Susan' relates to the pollution of Cheapside. In the nineteenth century, Charles Dickens's *Great Expectations* refers to the heavy traffic around Wood Street. In 1870, it was recorded that almost 12,000 vehicles passed along Cheapside in twenty-four hours. In the twentieth century, H G Wells's *Tono-Bungay* tells us that the roar of the traffic of Cheapside was 'stupendous'.

The antidote to this poisonous pocket of London is our lone tree. The plane is impervious to pollution. Indeed, it has been claimed that plane trees help remove up to 80% of city grime. The bark has pores to breathe through. When they become clogged with soot, the bark is shed in small patches. This gives it a unique speckled look at certain times of the year. The leaves are covered with hairs which also trap particles of soot. The hairs drop to the ground in summer to expose glossy clean leaves. The tree absorbs carbon dioxide and provides oxygen via the photosynthetic process, cleans the air, and provides shelter, shade and much-needed respite to its citizen neighbours.

Refugee and Migrant

The oldest retail premises in the City are three Cheapside shops built in 1687 which stand directly beneath the Wood Street plane. Despite the fact that the 'foreign' tree was planted over 130 years after the shops, they enjoy a symbiotic relationship; the lease of the properties forbids the building of another storey, allowing the tree to branch out. In turn, the tree's status is protected, which means developers cannot get their hands on the space around it, thus preventing the demolition of the shops.

Cheapside is London's oldest shopping street. The very name, from the old English *ceap*, meaning marketplace, made it synonymous with the shopping industry. The names of streets that run off it today are ghostly reminders of medieval trade: Bread Street, Milk Street, Honey Lane, Ironmonger Lane, Poultry etc.

During the sixteenth and seventeenth centuries, Cheapside was also London's main gold market. A gold refinery was based on Wood Street, and opposite to where the plane tree stands was Goldsmiths' Row, reputed to be the most finely decorated terrace of trading houses in the city. It featured images of woodmen carved in wood, financed by Thomas Wood, benefactor of St Peter Cheap church, who some say Wood Street is named after. The Great Fire of London in 1666 saw the Row's destruction and the decampment of the gold merchants, but Goldsmith Street, off Wood Street, still leads to the Goldsmiths' Hall, which stands on its original spot a block away.

During the nineteenth century, Cheapside lost practically all its retail business to the West End, particularly Oxford Street. However, under the tree's protective canopy, the three ancient shops soldiered on. Then, in 2010, the One New Change shopping centre opened, its angled brown glass reflecting not only the plane's green foliage but the full-scale return of Cheapside's time-honoured retail practice. In a successful homecoming, the old Wood Street plane, having seen the core business of the local community endure decades of decline, welcomed back trading neighbours on the site of the old Goldsmiths' Row.

Relic of History

The tree's canopy spreads over one of the most historic locations in the square mile, with its roots clawing deep into London's past. Signs of early civilisation at the tree's location date back to the last ice age. In the nineteenth century, twenty-five feet below the surface near the growing plane tree, workmen discovered the skull of a hunted wolf at least 10,000 years old. They subsequently found a bronze-age axe. The tree stands on the site of a 2,000-year-old Roman fort, and there are remnants of its wall nearby. According to the thirteenth-century chronicler Matthew Paris, the Anglo-Saxon King Offa (r. 757–96) had a royal palace next to St Alban's church in Wood Street.

From a medieval perspective, the tree stands on the site of the twelfth-century church St Peter Cheap, whose doors opened onto a major London landmark, the famous Cheapside Cross. Erected in 1290 to commemorate Queen Eleanor, the cross had been restored several times by the Tudor period. It was about thirty-six feet high with four levels of niches for small statues of monarchs, popes and saints, topped by a Greek cross. It bore a resemblance to the 'modern' cross that currently stands outside Charing Cross station. Combined with a public drinking fountain known as the Cheap Standard, it formed a boundary marker between the northern and southern city wards. It was used as a centrepiece for tournaments and pageants such as the Lord Mayor's show. It also became the focal point for visiting monarchs to the City of London. All royal proclamations in the City were read here. Indeed, Mary I was officially proclaimed queen here in 1553.

Sometime in the Elizabethan era, the Cheapside Cross began to give out a bad vibe. There were allegations, albeit from the puritanically minded, that it was a crucible of idolatry and devil worship. In 1581, an attack was made on the lower tier, and depictions of Christ, the Virgin Mary, the Resurrection and Edward the Confessor were all mutilated. Over the following decades, as a relic of the old religion, it became the focus of bitter controversy, eventually stirring active enmity. In 1641, a bishop compared the cross to the pagan deity Dagon, whose statue was destroyed by the power of the Ark of the Covenant which had been kept inside Dagon's temple (Samuel 1:5). The invocation of Dagon has a macabre local connection: the severed head of the biblical King Saul was also displayed in the temple of Dagon (Chronicles 1:10). Similarly, the head of the Scottish King James IV, slain at Flodden Field in 1513, was displayed at the house of a royal glazier who lived on Wood Street, and was later buried in the church of St Michael on the same thoroughfare.

The cross was attacked several more times as an agent of the devil before pamphlets were written in the voice of the cross itself. One has it relating its life story and current predicament to its sister, Charing Cross. Another, *The Doleful Lamentation of Cheapside Cross*, protests its innocence, accusing its attackers of greed, malice and lies. The cross then appears to curse the assailants with its revenge, telling them that even if it is destroyed, a 'rage' will continue to infect the assailants. The threat may have been taken seriously, as the following year the cross was actually denounced for treason! The puritan activist Richard Overton accused it of demonically seducing the people into disturbing the peace in his *Articles of High Treason Exhibited against Cheapside Cross* (1642). A major riot ensued when a group of apprentices, intent on bringing down the cross, were met by a group coming to its defence.

The Cheapside Cross continued to court controversy. Its impending doom was interpreted by some as a sign of the apocalypse. In some aspects, it might be seen as the catalyst for the Civil War in 1642. Certainly, it was a signal for the government-sanctioned iconoclasm of the period, as it was finally destroyed in 1643 by the Parliamentary Committee for the Demolition of Monuments of Superstition and Idolatry. 'And so, this Cross, poor Cross, all in a rage / They pulled down quite, the fault was only Age.'

Even after the Cheapside Cross was removed, it continued to haunt the minds of Londoners. Royalists continued to venerate the spot by removing their hats and crossing themselves, and a further pamphlet, *The Downfall of Dagon* (1643), personified the cross again, referring to 'his' death, funeral and legacies.

Not only can this location claim a role at the start of the Civil War, but also at the very end. In January 1661, while negotiations for the restoration of the monarchy were still ongoing, an armed group of fifty Anabaptist fanatics tried to capture the city. Known as the Fifth Monarchists, they took their name from a biblical prophecy that four monarchies, Babylonian, Persian, Macedonian and Roman, would precede the monarchy of Christ. They marched up Cheapside to the symbolic site of the Cheapside Cross. Here they were met by troops of the Trained Bands and the Life Guards. They were eventually corralled into

Wood Street, where a bloody pitched battle ensued. A heavy death toll saw twenty-two men killed. A further ten Fifth Monarchists were subsequently hanged, drawn and quartered. Three months later, Charles II was crowned king, with a royal proclamation announced here.

Shortly after the Restoration, citizens would have been mistaken in believing their apocalyptic punishment was over; a major outbreak of the deadly bubonic plague in 1665 coupled with the Great Fire a year later wreaked havoc in London. The parish clerks were licensed to keep the official death counts known as the Bills of Mortality. The Grim Reaper's toll was recorded at their company hall on Wood Street.

Rugged Emblem

As a pivot of Christian worship, few places in the medieval world could match Wood Street corner. Including St Peter Cheap, it boasted an incredible forty churches within a 300-yard radius, one of which, of course, was mighty St Paul.

St Peter Cheap, like the majority of these churches, was destroyed in the Great Fire. It was never rebuilt. Instead, this spiritual hub was turned into a small graveyard on which our plane tree was later planted. The surrounding railings date from 1712. Decorating these is the image of the crossed keys, signifying St Peter as the keeper of the gateway to Heaven.

In the Old Testament, Jesse was the father of King David. Isaiah 11:1 begins, 'There shall come forth a shoot from the stump of Jesse, and from this stem, a branch will bear fruit.' Medieval artists depicted Christ's ancestors in the form of a 'Jesse tree'.

The tripart symbolism of grave, tree and keeper also conjures an archaic pagan rite. In the ancient Roman world, wealthy families would bury their dead in a sacred wooded grove, then pay a 'keeper' to permanently watch over the graves. The lucrative nature of the 'king of the wood' meant he became a target of greed. Those with an eye on his handsome situation would signal a challenge by snapping a branch, the Golden Bough, from a tree in the grove to show that the current keeper was not worthy to hold the post. The keeper would then have to physically defend his livelihood. He constantly fought off these threats until he was inevitably usurped: the king is dead – long live the king. Thus the tree is a symbol of renewal.

Reaper of Stone

Under our plane tree lie the few remaining headstones from the original graveyard, their inscriptions fading. They include Obadiah Rogers, Hannah Canner and William Stapler. The Reverend Obadiah Wickes Rogers (d. 1816) was a 'Gentleman of Bermondsey' whose parents were parishioners here. Hannah Canner (d. 1808) was the wife of city marshal William Canner, who had died three years earlier after being infected by a diseased vagrant he was trying to remove from the parish. Three gun volleys were fired over the grave on his burial. William Stapler (d. 1810) was the uncle of John Stapler, who ran Wood Street's Cross Keys inn, deriving its name from St Peter's symbol. In Dickens's *Great Expectations*, Pip arrived at the inn to start a new life. Jeremiah Taverner is remembered in a stone plaque overlooking the graveyard. As a churchwarden, he oversaw the building of the adjacent shops in 1687.

Real-life Superhero

Moving on to the City's darkest days of all, the Blitz of World War II, this mystical place once again demonstrated its defiance in the face of adversity. The Wood Street plane survived a direct hit from a bomb in 1940.

POINT 11: ST PANCRAS GARDENS, PANCRAS ROAD

Route: Follow Cheapside westbound to St Paul's Cathedral. Continue westbound down Ludgate Hill to City Thameslink station. Take a train to St Pancras station. Leave via the western exit (Midland Road). Turn right and walk northbound along Midland Road and Pancras Road. St Pancras Gardens are on your right.

Here Lies ...

Here lies Adam's glory which 'shall never pass away'!
Here, though, come the martyr's icy fingers every May.

Here lies King Death's last hurrah with his subcommittees.
Here the dispossessed inherit the new rail of two cities.

Here lies an architect, in one of only two.
Here's the thing: it's his design, and we all share it too.

Here lies an immortal force; vampires; living dead.
Here romanticism breeds. Here, the wild get wed.

Here lies Mozart's mentor, remembered on a plaque.
Here is where we left him, and deigned to call him Back.

Here lies old faith ancestry; God bless 'em, every one.
Here sits Queen Bee's obelisk waiting for the sun.

Here lies a root of hope to countervail our dread:
Here grows high a Hardy tree to laurel all the dead.

St Pancras Gardens

St Pancras Old Church claims to be one of the oldest sites of Christian worship in the world. Pancras was a fourteen-year-old boy beheaded during the reign of Emperor Diocletian in the year 304. Some say a church was established here just ten years after his death, though this is disputed.

The parish of St Pancras practically stretched from the West End of London to Highgate. In 1822, the status of parish church passed to St Pancras New Church, which was consecrated on the New Road (Euston Road) half a mile away. However, St Pancras Old Church still operates as a place of worship today.

The church was rebuilt several times over the centuries. The seventeenth-century version was depicted in several prints in the early nineteenth century. At the gateway to the church sat the Adam and Eve tavern, which was demolished in the 1870s when the churchyard was formalised as a public park.

The last major reconstruction of the church was completed in 1848 by architect and local parishioner Alexander Gough. During these works, Roman tiles were revealed in the fabric, but ones that had been reused. They also found an inscribed altar stone dated to the year 625 and said to belong to St Augustine of Canterbury. According to archaeological expert Phil Emery, these elements suggest a Saxon foundation about three centuries later than originally claimed, but still of considerable antiquity.

Archaeological records show that the original graveyard design dated back to the church's Saxon period. Therefore, it must be regarded as one of the oldest Christian burial places in England.

The Ice Saints or *Saints de Glace,* St Mamertus, St Pancras and St Servatius, are so named because their feast days fall on the days of 11, 12 and 13 May respectively, roughly corresponding with the spring frosts that some gardeners dub 'the blackthorn winter'.

In 2005, I spoke to a surveyor from the St Pancras International construction project who was supervising the impact of the Eurostar rail extension on the churchyard. She told me that during excavations, several corpses had been dug up from what looked like a medieval plague pit. British workers refused to touch them, and foreign labour was used to exhume and relocate the bodies.

It has been asserted that many Roman Catholics were burnt here in Queen Elizabeth I's reign and that it became a favoured Catholic place of interment. Indeed, it is claimed that the last bell tolled for the old Catholic mass in England was at St Pancras.

In the 1650s, Oliver Cromwell's cavalry troops used the burial ground as a stable yard during the Civil War.

Jonathan Wild, 'Thief-Taker General', was buried alongside his wife in St Pancras churchyard in 1725, next to the church where they had been married four years earlier.

Wild is one of the most fascinating characters from the dark chapters of London's past. On the one hand, he formed an early skeleton of the modern police force, championing law and order as the self-proclaimed 'Thief-Taker General'. On the other, he was one of the most powerful overlords ever known in the world of organised crime.

Wild's 'Corporation of Thieves' comprised a huge army of crooks. In a great scam, they masqueraded as the returners of stolen goods at the Office of Recovery of Lost and Stolen Property. It was almost certain the goods were originally stolen by the gang members, and then ransomed back at a price. He also controlled a vast underworld network of spies, destroying all suspected rivals. He betrayed at least 120 men to hang, half of whom were his own accomplices. His evidence also helped to convict the popular rogue Jack Sheppard, whose defiance of Wild made him a hero. Wild was later caricatured as Peachum in John Gay's *Beggar's Opera*, with Sheppard the original inspiration behind 'Mack the Knife'.

Wild was convicted and hanged for stealing lace! Shortly after his burial, his body was dug up and sold for dissection. Today his skeleton is on display at the Hunterian Museum, inside the Royal College of Surgeons, which sits directly opposite Sir John Soane's Museum in Lincoln's Inn Fields.

Somewhere in the churchyard lie the remains of the German composer Johann Christian Bach (1735–82). The youngest son of J S Bach, his own contribution to music is immeasurable: during the 1760s he spent several years in London teaching one of the greatest composers of all, Mozart. Despite his legacy, J C Bach's body rests in an unknown pauper's grave. All we have to remind us of his burial here is a faded inscription on a small grey stone plaque. It's propped up against a railing. Meanwhile, his name is lazily spelt in the burial register as John Cristian Back.

The founder of modern feminism, Mary Wollstonecraft, married the philosopher William Godwin at St Pancras Old Church. Author of *A Vindication of the Rights of Women*, she was also buried here in 1797 after she died from complications brought on during the birth of her daughter Mary. Seventeen years later, it is said that the Romantic poet Percy Bysshe Shelley fell in love with Mary Godwin after assignations at her mother's grave, and planned their elopement to Switzerland. Mary Shelley's *Frankenstein*, published shortly afterwards, was partly inspired by her visits to this graveyard. A memorial tomb for Mary Wollstonecraft and William Godwin still remains, though their true graves are now in St Peter's church, Bournemouth.

St Pancras churchyard has always had a strong French connection. In the early nineteenth century, a large number of refugees, driven from France during the revolution, were buried here. Amongst them were several French bishops, noblemen and diplomats.

In the 1820s, vampire writer and physician John Polidori was buried in St Pancras churchyard, as was the great sculptor John Flaxman, a man who made heroes immortal.

Sir John Soane (1753–1837) was a classical architect who obsessively collected relics of buildings past, as can be seen in his peculiar labyrinthine museum in Lincoln's Inn Fields. In St Pancras churchyard he built an impressive mausoleum for the burial of his beloved wife and was later interred in it himself. The mausoleum is one of only two Grade I listed funerary monuments in London (the other being Karl Marx's tomb in Highgate). The structure's canopy inspired the twentieth-century architect Giles Gilbert Scott in his design for the roof of the famous red telephone box.

Charles Dickens made the churchyard the location of a body-snatching scene in his 1859 novel *A Tale of Two Cities*, set in London and Paris at the time of the French Revolution. The gravestone of Dickens's former schoolmaster William Jones can also be found here. He was the inspiration for Mr Creakle, the cruel headmaster of Salem House in *David Copperfield*.

The churchyard grew considerably over the centuries and was enlarged several times, particularly during the post-medieval period as London morphed into a monster metropolis. There was a major expansion between 1792 and 1802 when the church of St Giles-in-the-Fields acquired the adjacent land as a burial ground extension. By the 1850s, the necropolis around St Pancras Old Church stretched across eight acres.

Both graveyards were closed for burials in 1854. In the early 1860s, the Midland Railway were laying the foundations for the new St Pancras station. The company got permission to drive their tracks directly through the old graveyard without necessarily removing thousands of buried remains. A public outcry forced the Bishop of London to ask architect Arthur Blomfeld, designer of London's Royal College of Music and himself the son of a former Bishop of London, to exhume and remove the bodies before the construction.

In 1865, Blomfeld employed his assistant, the young novelist Thomas Hardy, to supervise this work. Struggling for space on the limited hallowed ground he had been given, Hardy arranged for some of the headstones from the disturbed graves to be placed in a circle around an ash tree in St Pancras churchyard. One evening, Blomfeld and Hardy watched as a coffin disintegrated, revealing a skeleton with two skulls. Years later, when they met again, Blomfeld reminded the now-established writer about the incident: 'Do you remember how we found the man with two heads at St Pancras?''

Queen bee refers to Baroness Angela Burdett-Coutts, one of the richest women of the nineteenth century. The banking heiress, also known as the Queen of the Poor, ploughed much of her own personal fortune into a variety of philanthropic causes, including women's employment and education, child welfare, animal protection, military hospitals and international relief projects.

Burdett-Coutts helped the poverty-stricken of London by building new housing and public spaces. She oversaw the conversion of disused or dilapidated burial grounds into gardens for local residents, including the churchyard of St Pancras Old Church. Here she presented an impressive fountain and sundial (now Grade II listed) as a memorial to graves lost in the clearances.

In the summer of 1968, the Beatles reunited for the first time in several months to record the White Album. The famous opening lyrics, 'Hey, Jude, don't be afraid . . .' were about to be conveyed to the world, and, as part of a promotional shoot, the band visited St Pancras churchyard with the renowned photographer Don McCullin.

The session, which became known as the Beatles' Mad Day Out, included various poses near the gates, the drinking fountain, Soane's tomb, the church doorway, flowerbeds and various benches. A plaque on one of the benches reads, 'John, George, Paul and Ringo from the Beatles sat here during their Mad Day Out, July 28, 1968.' Unfortunately, the Beatles did not 'come together' for very long, and soon after this shoot they began to fragment. Indeed, Ringo had actually left the band by the time 'Hey Jude' was released a month later, although he subsequently rejoined.

It is claimed John Lennon had written 'I Am the Walrus' and 'Glass Onion' several months earlier in deliberate response to fans who looked for hidden messages in their lyrics. 'Glass Onion' was the first track recorded as a full band after Ringo rejoined. The lyrics suggested that Paul McCartney was symbolised by the walrus. In 2013, construction workers on the St Pancras International project discovered the remains of a walrus in a coffin while clearing the graveyard. No one has been able to fully explain how it came to be there.

St Pancras International station became the terminal for the London to Paris rail line in 2007. The opening was commemorated at St Pancras Old Church with a bilingual service and a twinning with the church of Saint-Vincent-de-Paul near the Gare du Nord, Paris.

In 2009, a stone sculpture was placed at the entrance to the church. Created by the artist Emily Young, it was inscribed, 'And I am here, in a place beyond desire or fear': an extract from the poem 'Praise' by Jeremy Clarke.

POINT 12: KENWOOD HOUSE, HAMPSTEAD LANE

Route: Return to St Pancras station and take the Northern line underground to Hampstead station. Walk northbound along Heath Street, then take the right fork along Spaniards Road and Hampstead Lane. Follow to Kenwood House.

Afterwards, return to St Pancras station, the nearest major transport hub. With the postscript in mind, you may wish to hail an iconic London black cab to do this.

Eden

I rode the line of misery, against an inner voice,
'Twixt Balaam and the Angel, with little other choice.
Just a little further on – knee-deep in freebie news
And smoking-cough late risers – emerged from blackened hues.
You cannot flash yer Hampsteads without a bluish plaque
Of pioneering vagueness, an army stretching back.
Their motors squeeze the Spaniards (built in 1593).
'Is this the way to Kenwood, mate? Where Dido was set free?'
The architectural apple of Adam's eye is there.

He built a place of happiness for Mickey and Jack Bear,
Merlin's wizard rollerskates must have been quite nifty.
They also did a breakfast for only £6.50.
In Repton's red-book rhapsody, the rays of spring were blinking.
How many miserable journeys end in Eden? I was thinking.

Kenwood House

'Eden' reflects a journey to visit Kenwood House in Hampstead, north London, using the London Underground Northern line (known by some as the 'misery line') from Balham to Hampstead via Angel.

Hampstead has some impressive residences, but it seems to me there is a slight 'keeping up with the Joneses' aspect to the proliferation of blue plaques, with many dedicated to slightly obscure historical figures.

Along the Spaniards Road, where the road curves and narrows into Hampstead Lane, sits the Spaniards inn. The structure was built in the 1580s but first operated as an inn during the early eighteenth century. Some say the famous highwayman Dick Turpin used the Spaniards as a hideout, and apparently he still does, as his ghost is rumoured to haunt the bar where there is a framed pistol ball 'fired by him'.

The inn has many artistic connections. The Romantic poets Blake, Byron and Keats are all said to have drunk here. Indeed, Keats's famous 'Ode to a Nightingale' is said to have been written at the inn. British rock band the Faces claim to have formed at the Spaniards.

The Spaniards inn faces the grounds of Kenwood House. This historic residence was designed in the eighteenth century by the architect Robert Adam, with gardens by Humphry Repton. A place with superb views of London, its beauty made 'Mickey and Jack Bear' very happy, according to a plaque on a garden bench.

The black slave girl Dido Elizabeth Belle lived at Kenwood House for thirty-one years. Born in 1761, the daughter of British naval officer Sir John Lindsay, she was adopted by his uncle, the 1st Earl of Mansfield, who owned Kenwood House. As Lord Chief Justice he presided over several notable trials that influenced the abolitionist cause. Dido Belle was officially granted freedom on his death in 1793.

After complaints from Hampstead residents in 2006, Kenwood sadly ended its famous series of classical summer concerts.

POSTSCRIPT

Psyche Central

I came suddenly upon such knotty problems of alleys, such enigmatical entries, and such sphynx's riddles of streets without thoroughfares, as must, I conceive, baffle the audacity of porters and confound the intellects of hackney-coachmen.

These lines from De Quincey's *Confessions* remind me of a London pressure point that is now lost forever. The Public Carriage Office is the administrative bureau for the city's black cab trade. For many years it was hidden away from public gaze, housed in a dull, grey, three-storey, concrete sixties office block, on Penton Street, a relatively featureless side road in a north London suburb.

So far, the psychogeographic links aren't promising. At a stretch, one might note that close by is the Angel, Islington, where, during the 1930s, London was remapped in the shape of a board game (Monopoly). Or that the PCO has since moved to 212 Baker Street, opposite the fictitious address of Sherlock Holmes: in hailing a cab, perhaps the most pertinent literary spot in the world.

But the Penton Street building was much more intrinsically linked with the notion of psychogeography. For almost half a century, prospective cabbies would regularly attend 'appearances' here. This fifteen-minute test is the culmination of many months of intense religious study of London's streets and marks a stage in the student's long quest to complete 'The Knowledge'.

The candidate, smartly dressed, sits opposite a stern examiner (always respectfully addressed as 'Sir' or 'Ma'am'), who will begin by randomly selecting any two points on a London map. The candidate must then orally relay the fastest route between those points, noting the names of every street *en route* and the correct left or right turns used. Next, the examiner might ask for the address of any one of the thousands of pubs, restaurants, hotels, attractions or points of interest in the London area, and will expect the candidate to know the answer. The examiner might finish with another A-to-B route.

A good 'appearance' would earn you the points required for a shimmy up the ladder in pursuit of the coveted cabbie badge. A bad one sent you slip-sliding back to start that stage all over again. Either way, a harrowing experience.

But the real dread lay elsewhere. On the first floor of this office block was a long room, down one side of which was a line of twelve black seats. This was where candidates sat nervously waiting for their appearance, and it was a place of pure intimidation. The seats were arranged to face a gigantic scale map of Greater London. So vast, it covered the entire wall, and so detailed that it depicted every one of the 60,000(!) streets. Here, London was the veritable Prince of Darkness. Exactly how many thousands were cowed by sheer terror in that literal nerve centre will remain a mystery, but not for nothing was this place known in cabbie lore as 'Old Death Row'. Psychogeography indeed.

ROMANCING THE BRITISH MUSEUM

Exploring how English poetry reflected this cultural institution at the height of imperialism

A sunny day in London Town
Perked me up when I was down.
I viewed the morning with great calm.
The British Museum had found its charm.

INTRODUCTION

The British Museum: the world's greatest collection of antiquities. Seven million objects spanning two million years of human history and covering over one million square feet of floor space – right in the heart of London.

A Little Psychogeography

The museum's advantageous location was the result of a little providence. The story begins in the 1670s when the Duke of Montagu decided to build a townhouse on the newly laid-out Great Russell Street in Bloomsbury. It was completed in 1678 by Robert Hooke and, after a fire seven years later, rebuilt by the French architect Pouget. The site was quite literally on the northern edge of London, at the very apex of a right angle, equidistant from the beating hearts of two cities: Westminster (the power) and London (the money). Beyond it lay only fields all the way to Highgate and Hampstead.

By the turn of the eighteenth century, the rear of the site had already become an attraction for visitors. Tradition has it that sometime in the 1680s two brothers killed each other here in a duel over a woman, and the impressions of their last steps were said to have been imprinted on the ground. Thus it became known as the Field of the Forty Footsteps.

In 1732, a shadow was cast onto the front of Montagu House with the completion of the 150-foot pyramidical spire of St George Bloomsbury: the last church built by the architect Nicholas Hawksmoor, and some say his best.

His dominating design was based on the Mausoleum of Halicarnassus. This ancient structure was built as a tomb for King Mausolus, the fourth-century BC ruler of the Greek province of Charia (in modern-day Turkey). It was regarded as one of the seven wonders of the ancient world. Hawksmoor had never seen the original building. Indeed, it had lain in ruins since a thirteenth-century earthquake. He used the dimensions recorded by the first-century Roman writer Pliny the Elder. Like the original, Hawksmoor augmented his pyramidical spire with heraldic beasts, and, also like the original, he had the church orientated on a north-south axis, against ecclesiastical authority.

A hundred and twenty-five years later, the British Museum heralded the arrival of a statue of King Mausolus which had fallen from the original Mausoleum. The effigy of the ancient king was re-erected after an epic journey: 2,200 years after his death, 1,700 miles from his original realm, in a city that, when he ruled, didn't even exist. Yet, with pure synchronicity, just yards from Hawksmoor's pyramidical tribute.

During the 1750s, the first trustees of the British Museum hunted for a space large enough to display their growing acquisitions. The embryonic collection of over 70,000 specimens was the legacy of Sir Hans Sloane (1660–1753). Irish botanist, royal physician and president of the Royal Society (following Sir Isaac Newton), he had spent his lifetime accumulating and classifying objects.

In 1756, the Montagu family decided to sell their townhouse, partly due to the construction of a busy London bypass (the New Road) 800 yards to the north, and partly due to being in close proximity to one of the worst slums in London, the Rookery. This ghetto had an evil reputation. The western edge was by the church of St Giles-in-the-Fields. The Great Plague of London had started here in 1665. St George Bloomsbury marked the eastern edge. The whole district – with Hawksmoor's spire prominent in the background – was famously depicted in William Hogarth's 1751 print *Gin Lane*, exposing the area's deprivation and depravity to the world at large.

The buyer of Montagu House was the British Museum. Thus its doors, when first opened in 1759, separated the world of highest human endeavour from the lowest human squalor. Perhaps partly in response, the early trustees took great pride in adopting an altruistic outlook: not only was the museum to be the first 'British' public institution, but it was also decreed the collection would belong to the citizens of the world as a free right (a radical concept back then).

A few years after the museum opened, London experienced the greatest outbreak of civil unrest in its history: the week-long Gordon Riots in 1780. To quell the upheaval, the authorities set up seven key military camps around the capital. They were all sited at major non-religious institutions: the Tower of London, Bank Junction, Lincoln's Inn, Somerset House, Charing Cross, Whitehall, and the youngest recruit at just twenty-one years old, the British Museum. Indeed, the museum and Somerset House were the chief strategic sentinels, flanking the axis that effectively divided the city into equal halves. This call to action may well have saved the museum's collection from the large-scale looting during the disturbances.

At the dawn of the nineteenth century, the museum's seat on London's northern boundary was under threat and gradually surrounded by development. Then, in the 1850s, architect Robert Smirke redesigned the museum as a purpose-built space. His younger brother Sydney completed the neoclassical-styled building before a north side extension was added in 1912. By then, the Natural History Museum had been established in Kensington to cater to the animal, vegetable and mineral side of the collection, leaving the British Museum to concentrate on its role as civilisation's hall of fame.

Celebration Versus Sorrow

Over its 260-year existence, the British Museum has attracted around half a billion visitors. It has also inspired an army of dreamers to wax lyrical. Some took inspiration from working full-time at the museum, such as the 'Library Poets' Edmund Gosse, Arthur O'Shaughnessy, Coventry Patmore and the self-styled 'darling of the British Museum Reading Room', Theo Marzials. Others, such as the great Romantics Byron, Keats and Shelley, found poetic licence in the exhibits themselves. Later luminaries such as Rossetti, Hardy and Yeats were also stirred to record their admiration of objects in verse. Such descriptive narrative, a form of art imitating art, is known as *ekphrasis*.

The juxtaposition of exotic arts and antiquities in a 'neutral' setting provoked several conflicts for poets. Among the arguments: shouldn't ancient artefacts remain nobly in situ to be respectfully viewed by the passing cultured visitor? Isn't it an act of desecration or vandalism to forcibly remove such antiquities from their original surroundings? Isn't it an act of theft for one nation to appropriate the cultural treasures of another? Isn't the 'captivity' of such plunder against a liberal ethos?

Countering those: isn't it elitist to suggest that ancient artefacts can and should only be appreciated by the cultured visitor who can afford to travel to view them? Aren't these antiquities crumbling into ruin in their original surroundings? Wouldn't it be better to conserve them in a safe environment for future generations to admire and learn from? Indeed, isn't it the very nature of the museum that allows for the existence of the exhibits within, and isn't it that very existence that gives everyone, including poets, the freedom and opportunity to appreciate these treasures?

In his book *Poetic Exhibitions*, Eric Gidal calls this conflict the aesthetic ambivalence between celebration and sorrow. The most famous example in the museum comes with the Parthenon sculptures, more famously known as the Elgin Marbles. In the early nineteenth century, Lord Elgin prepared to export sizable chunks of the ruined Acropolis from Athens to London. For some, it constituted nothing less than the rape of ancient Greek culture. Lord Byron led the condemnation in his poems 'The Curse of Minerva' (1811) and 'Childe Harold's Pilgrimage' (1812–18), where he saw a roughshod disrespect for the past: 'Stop! For thy tread is on an Empire's dust!'

A Moral Maze

The existential value of antiquities was also bought into question, for, when castrated from the context of time and place in a remote display case with a few descriptive words, an object's history becomes disengaged. The quote 'Once you label me, you negate me' comes to mind. John Keats felt that the preservation of such antiquities could provoke an existential crisis of the soul: a reminder of your own mortality and gradual decay of your life's work. Keats suffered these feelings in 'On Seeing the Elgin Marbles' (1817):

> *Such dim-conceived glories of the brain*
> *Bring round the heart an indescribable feud;*
> *So do these wonders a most dizzy pain,*
> *That mingles Grecian grandeur with the rude*
> *Wasting of old time . . .*

The 'Is nothing sacred?' attitude may appear to constitute the classic response to such exhibits during the Romantic period. But in fact many contemporaries saw themselves as the rightful appropriators of such antiquities on behalf of the young expanding British empire, which they saw as the natural heir apparent to the ancient empires of Egypt, Greece and Rome. In an edition of the *Examiner*, the literary critic William Hazlitt recommended the sculptures be acquired by Britain to 'lift the fine arts out of the limbo of vanity and affectation'.

There is no doubt that the eventual arrival of the sculptures in London marked a watershed moment in the study of art. For the first time in a public arena in their own country, the British people saw *originals* of Greek statues, not copies. The Royal Academy painter Benjamin West championed their acquisition, claiming they would serve as models for his own epic paintings. Byron, it may be noted, had already savaged him in 'The Curse of Minerva': 'The flattering, feeble dotard, West, Europe's worst dauber, and poor Britain's best ...'

'Modern Greece' (1817) is Felicia Hemans's riposte to Byron and his criticism of West. She suggests that the sculptures could serve as an inspiration for contemporary art: 'And who can tell how pure, how bright a flame, caught from these models, may illume the west? What British Angelo may rise to fame?' Hemans's point mirrors Eric Gidal's assertion that the glory of the British empire was manifest in the *exhibition* of the sculptures: if they can inspire new art in Britain, in the Brave New World, or in future cultures, then ekphrasis trumps ethics.

In another direct response to Byron, Hemans espied the opportunity for the museum to act as a cherished time capsule where future generations would benefit: 'All that hath lived, while empires have expired ...'

A flip side to this 'new dawn' was the notion that, one day, modern empires too would expire. This sentiment was mooted by the French philosopher de Volney in his *Ruins of Empires* (1802): 'Who knows if on the banks of ... the Thames ... some traveller, like myself, shall not one day sit on their silent ruins, and weep in solitude over the ashes of their inhabitants, and the memory of their former greatness.' Horace Smith in 'Leg of Granite' (1817) took up the mantle, suggesting the existential meaning of artefacts could be blurred in a distant future: 'Some hunter may express wonder like ours, when through the wilderness where London stood, holding the wolf in chase, he meets some fragment huge, and stops to guess what powerful, but unrecorded, race once dwelt in that annihilated place.' Rossetti's 'The Burden of Nineveh' (1856) went further, pondering a future civilisation, perhaps Australian, plundering the ruins of the museum and presuming the Assyrian bull was actually a relic of London: 'Some tribe of the Australian plough bear him afar, – a relic now of London, not of Nineveh.'

Taking the past as a perspective, some poets tried to evoke the psychogeographic power of exhibits by conjuring up the ghosts of antiquity and projecting them via a portal from their original site to the British Museum. Rossetti, again in 'The Burden of Nineveh', imagines the characters who once found shade under the Assyrian bulls: 'Within thy shadow, haply, once Sennacherib has knelt ...' Similarly, Thomas Hardy in 'In the British Museum' (1919) contemplates the echoes of time as he inspects the base of a pillar from the Athens court from which St Paul apparently preached: 'But I am thinking that stone has echoed the voice of Paul ...'

Rossetti also reflects that some ancient artefacts, however clinically displayed, are incongruously positioned and crudely pitched against each other. This competition for attention results in lost mystique.

> *While school-foundations in the act*
> *Of holiday, three files compact,*
> *Shall learn to view thee as a fact*
> *Connected with that zealous tract:*
> *Rome, Babylon and Nineveh ...*
>
> *Greece, Egypt, Rome, did any god*
> *Before whose feet men knelt unshod*
> *Deem that in this unblessed abode*
> *Another scarce more unknown god*
> *Should house with him, from Nineveh? ...*
>
> *And now, they and their gods and thou,*
> *All relics here together now ...*

Guilt, pride, cultural negation, progressive hegemony, disillusioned ambition, spiritual continuity. The British Museum was quite literally a moral maze for poets to ponder. Yet generations of them were collectively drawn to this London institution, chiefly captivated by the splendid isolation of antiquities, and the opportunities it provided for translating such artistic wonders into artistic words.

Note: A shorter, edited version of this essay entitled 'The British Museum Gets Lyrical' formed an official British Museum blog to commemorate National Poetry Day in 2017.

POINT 1: GREAT COURT

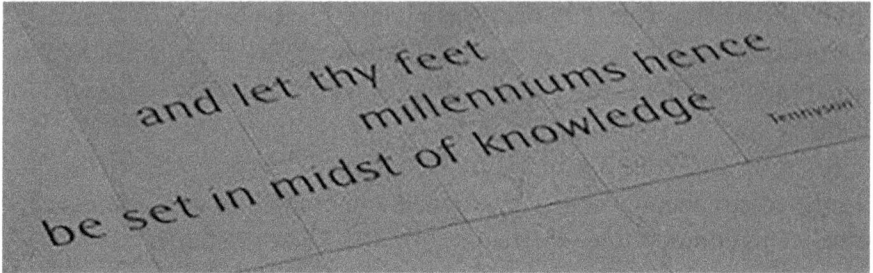

Route: Enter museum via front entrance. Pass through foyer into the Great Court. The inscription from Tennyson's 'The Two Voices' is on the floor near the base of the right-hand staircase around the old Reading Room.

Alfred Lord Tennyson, 'The Two Voices' (1833) (extracts)

A still small voice spake unto me,
'Thou art so full of misery,
Were it not better not to be?'

'Forerun thy peers, thy time, and let
Thy feet, millenniums hence, be set
In midst of knowledge, dreamed not yet.'

And I arose, and I released
The casement, and the light increased
With freshness in the dawning east.

On to God's house the people pressed:
Passing the place where each must rest,
Each entered like a welcome guest.

One walked between his wife and child,
With measured footfall firm and mild,
And now and then he gravely smiled.

These three made unity so sweet,
My frozen heart began to beat,
Remembering its ancient heat.

A second voice was at mine ear,
A little whisper silver-clear,
A murmur, 'Be of better cheer.'

So heavenly-toned, that in that hour
From out my sullen heart a power
Broke, like the rainbow from the shower

To feel, although no tongue can prove,
That every cloud, that spreads above
And veileth love, itself is love.

Comprising two acres, the Great Court within the British Museum is one of the largest covered public areas in the world. Originally designed by Robert Smirke as a courtyard garden, it was recently transformed by Foster and Partners to commemorate the millennium. It is crowned by a magnificent 900-ton roof made of steel girders and over 3,300 reflective glass triangles.

On the floor of the Great Court, near the base of the right-hand staircase that sweeps up around the old Reading Room, you will see the inscription 'and let thy feet millenniums hence be set in midst of knowledge', a quote from the poem 'The Two Voices' by the poet Alfred (Lord) Tennyson (1809–92).

Tennyson wrote 'The Two Voices' when he was just twenty-four. It is an intense poem about the insignificance of man compared to the infinite scale of universal knowledge. So the quote seems perfect for the environment. However, the poem was originally titled 'Thoughts of a Suicide', and written while Tennyson was in a deep depression. The full line is 'Forerun your peers, your time, and let thy feet, millenniums hence, be set in midst of knowledge, dreamed not yet.' In other words, the quote reflects the poet's inner voice tempting him to end it all. To die now in the hope of reincarnation in more enlightened times. Tennyson said, 'When I wrote it, I was so utterly miserable, a burden to myself and to my family, that I said, "Is life worth anything?"' Thankfully, the grim narrative of the work concludes with hope and salvation. The poet spies a family happily out walking, then marvels at the beauty of nature. His heart rejoices in the answer to all his fears: all you need is love.

POINT 2: READING ROOM

Route: The Reading Room is viewed from the outside. The inside can only be accessed by purchasing a ticket for an exhibition held therein.

Edward Carpenter, 'In the British Museum Library' (1883) (extracts)

How lovely! This vast, vast dome – and the suspended sounds within it!
Sounds and echoes of the great city vibrating tirelessly night and day;
Voices and footfalls, of the little creatures that walk about its floor, half-lost in the
*   huge concave;*
Suspended whispers, from its walls, of far forgotten centuries.

Come, come away! leave books, traditions, all the dross of centuries,
Clean, clean thy wings, and fly through other worlds.
Heaven's stars shine all around thee;
Deep in thy Heart the ageless celestial Museum
Waits its explorer. All that they said – those wise ones –
They say and repeat it now, where the plough-boy drives his furrow:
Be still, O Soul, and know that thou art God.

Louise Imogen Guiney, 'In the Reading-Room of the British Museum' (1893)

Praised be the moon of books! that doth above
A world of men, the fallen Past behold,
And fill the spaces else so void and cold
To make a very heaven again thereof;
As when the sun is set behind a grove,
And faintly unto nether ether rolled,
All night his whiter image and his mould
Grows beautiful with looking on her love.

Thou therefore, moon of so divine a ray,
Lend to our steps both fortitude and light!
Feebly along a venerable way
They climb the infinite, or perish quite;
Nothing are days and deeds to such as they,
While in this liberal house thy face is bright.

The circular structure in the heart of the Great Court was once the seventh incarnation of the Reading Room, operating as the national library. It was completed in 1857 by Sidney Smirke based on designs by chief librarian Antonio Panizzi. With twenty-five miles of shelving holding 1.3 million books and accommodating over 300 readers, it was in operation for 150 years. In 1997, a space issue saw the library moved to new premises about a mile away. As part of the Great Court redevelopment, the room was turned into a public research centre and exhibition space.

Despite being a shadow of its former self, the room's psychogeographic power should not be dismissed. Its influence on global political thinking is immeasurable. Sylvia Pankhurst shaped her campaign for women's suffrage here. Nationalists such as Mahatma Gandhi and Giuseppe Garibaldi studied here, as did Communist thinkers Ho Chi Minh, Vladimir Lenin, Leon Trotsky and Karl Marx, the last of whom came here almost every day for thirty years while writing *Das Kapital*. Indeed, Soviet president Mikhail Gorbachev suggested this place should shoulder the 'blame' for Marxism.

In the pantheon of English literature, it is a legendary place, and any writer worth their salt has used it. The greatest poets from the past two centuries spent hours polishing lines here, including Matthew Arnold, Rupert Brooke, Robert Browning, T S Eliot, Rudyard Kipling, Edward Lear, John Masefield, Christina Rossetti, Oscar Wilde and W B Yeats. They sat at the same desks as novelists Sir Arthur Conan Doyle, Joseph Conrad, Charles Dickens, George Eliot, E M Forster, Graham Greene, Thomas Hardy, Aldous Huxley, Jerome K Jerome, George Orwell, Beatrix Potter, Bram Stoker, William Makepeace Thackeray, Mark Twain, H G Wells and Virginia Woolf. Some of the world's greatest fictional characters were born here, such as Ebenezer Scrooge, Count Dracula and Sherlock Holmes. Irish playwright George Bernard Shaw considered his research here the equivalent of a university education. When he died in 1950, he bequeathed the museum a generous share of his legacy, swelled by the popularity of his works such as *Pygmalion*.

Some writers used the room as a plot location. Max Beerbohm's short story 'Enoch Soames' (1916) is about a writer who in 1897 wishes to know if posterity will remember him. He makes a pact with the devil to transport him to the Reading Room exactly one hundred years in the future (1997 – eerily the year it closed). First to use it as a location was George Gissing in *New Grub Street* (1891). Here, a female reader, Marian Yule, makes constant visits to the room biblically described as the 'valley of the shadow of books'. In the same novel, Gissing observes how peculiarly oppressive the atmosphere was, causing headaches and coughs.

David Lodge, in *The British Museum Is Falling Down* (1965), remarks how the stale air was sealed in and the 'faint, sour smell of mouldering books and bindings was like the reek of rotting vegetation in some fetid oriental backwater'. English poet Richard Aldington notes the 'heavy musty air' in his poem 'At the British Museum' (1929). In 1868, the poet A C Swinburne was overwhelmed by inhaling the stifling air and fainted in the room, nearly dying according to his contemporary Edmund Gosse. An appearance by Swinburne here was the subject for poet laureate John Masefield's last poem 'The Reading Room' (1966).

The vast weight of knowledge could also be intimidating, prompting bouts of lethargy, ennui and despair. The Irish poet W B Yeats compiled his *Irish Fairy Tales* and a two-volume work on Irish novelists here. In his memoirs, *The Trembling of the Veil* (1922), he remembers avoiding some books simply because they were too heavy: 'I spent my days at the British Museum and must, I think, have been delicate, for I remember often putting off hour after hour consulting some necessary book because I shrank from lifting the heavy volumes of the catalogue.' David Lodge also picked up on this characteristic in *The British Museum Is Falling Down*: 'He would sit slumped at his desk at the British Museum, a heap of neglected books before him.'

Another aspect was the 'scruffy' nature of readers. Charles Dickens in 'Shabby-Genteel People' from *Sketches by Boz* (1836) describes an encounter: 'He first attracted our notice by sitting opposite to us in the reading-room at the British Museum. There he used to sit all day, as close to the table as possible, in order to conceal the lack of buttons on his coat: with his old hat carefully deposited at his feet.' Later, the man attempts to improve the appearance of his suit by temporarily reviving it with 'blacking' liquid. Dickens, having worked in a blacking factory as a young boy, spots the deceit.

George Gissing visits this theme in *New Grub Street*: 'His garb must have seen a great deal of Museum service; it consisted of a jacket, something between brown and blue, hanging in capacious shapelessness, a waistcoat half-open for lack of buttons and with one of the pockets coming unsewn, a pair of bronze-hued trousers which had all run to knee ...' And David Lodge in *The British Museum Is Falling Down* has one of his characters remark, 'He's going to become one of the museum eccentrics. Before we know it, he'll be shuffling around in slippers and muttering into his beard.' Anglo-African poet William Plomer also picked up on the untidiness of readers in 'A Ticket for the Reading Room' (1940).

The domed roof reinforces the psychophysical nature of the Reading Room. Made from cast iron and glass, and 140 feet in diameter, it was, when completed in 1857, the world's second-largest dome after the Pantheon in Rome. Crowning the sum of encyclopaedic knowledge below, its resemblance to the human brain was not lost. Virginia Woolf referred to it in her essay 'A Room of One's Own' (1929): 'There one stood under the vast dome, as if one were a thought in the huge bald forehead which is so splendidly encircled by a band of famous names.' David Lodge, in *The British Museum Is Falling Down*, went further: 'It was like a diagram of something – a brain or a nervous system, and the foreshortened people moving about in irregular clusters were like blood corpuscles or molecules.' The oppressive cocoon-like atmosphere, the lethargic nature of the readers, and the brain comparisons are brought together by the Irish romantic poet Louis MacNeice in 'The British Museum Reading Room' (1939).

When the web-like glass roof was added to the Great Court at the turn of the millennium, aerial shots revealed the dome now appeared a physical example of Einstein's 'geodetic effect', a semi-submerged planetary mass warping the fabric of universal space-time around it. The celestial nature of the Reading Room had already been ekphrastically noted. The English philosopher-poet Edward Carpenter (1844–1929) called it a 'huge concave' of a world lost within a universe in his poem 'In the British Museum Library', whilst the traditionalist American poet and essayist Louise Imogen Guiney (1861–1920) echoed the astronomical theme, describing it as an illuminating 'moon' in her 'In the Reading-Room of the British Museum' (1893).

POINT 3:
KING'S LIBRARY/ENLIGHTENMENT
GALLERY (ROOM 1)

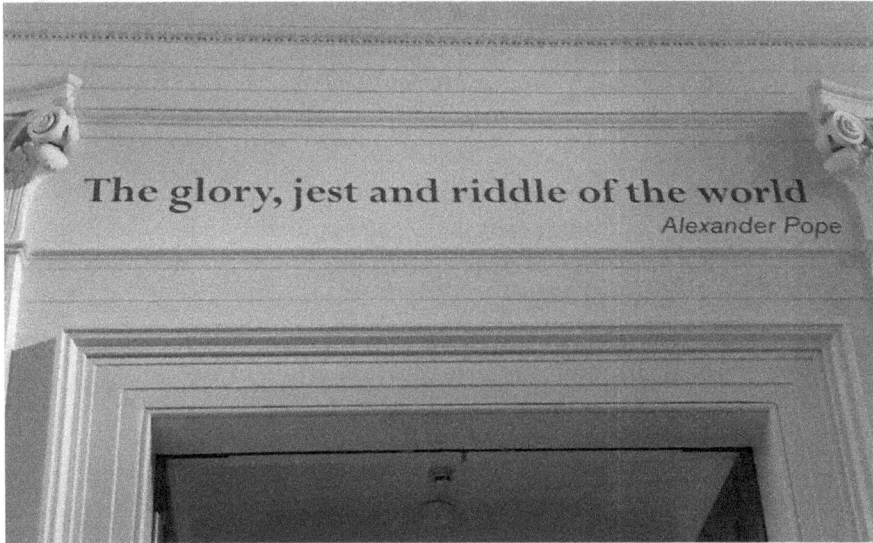

The glory, jest and riddle of the world
Alexander Pope

Route: Enter the King's Library from the Great Court (to the right of the Reading Room). The inscription from Pope's 'Essay on Man' is on the entablature above the south entrance to the King's Library.

Alexander Pope, 'An Essay on Man' (1732–34) (extracts)

Say first, of God above, or man below,
What can we reason, but from what we know?
Of man what see we, but his station here,
From which to reason, or to which refer?

Hope springs eternal in the human breast:
Man never is, but always to be blest:
The soul, uneasy and confined from home,
Rests and expatiates in a life to come.

All are but parts of one stupendous whole,
Whose body Nature is, and God the soul;
That, changed through all, and yet in all the same,
Great in the earth, as in the ethereal frame,

Know then thyself, presume not God to scan,
The proper study of mankind is man.
Placed on this isthmus of a middle state,
A being darkly wise, and rudely great:

Alike in ignorance, his reason such,
Whether he thinks too little, or too much;
Chaos of thought and passion, all confused;
Still by himself, abused or disabused;

Created half to rise and half to fall;
Great lord of all things, yet a prey to all,
Sole judge of truth, in endless error hurled;
The glory, jest and riddle of the world.

Go, wondrous creature! mount where science guides,
Go, measure earth, weigh air, and state the tides;
Instruct the planets in what orbs to run,
Correct old time, and regulate the sun;

Go, soar with Plato to the empyreal sphere,
To the first good, first perfect, and first fair;
Or tread the mazy round his followers trod,
And quitting sense call imitating God;

As Eastern priests in giddy circles run,
And turn their heads to imitate the sun.
Go, teach Eternal Wisdom how to rule –
Then drop into thyself, and be a fool!

In 1837, a purpose-built room was completed in the museum to hold the royal collection of books donated by King George III. It subsequently became known as the King's Library and is the oldest part of the museum as it stands today. At 300ft in length, 30ft wide and 40ft high, it was designed in the neoclassical style. Regarded as one of the finest rooms in London, it is something of an exhibit in itself.

The theme of the artefacts within the King's Library is the culmination of the 'Enlightenment' or 'Age of Reason' which blossomed between 1650 and 1800, following on from the Renaissance and Reformation in Europe. Enlightenment philosophy questioned traditional, classical or religious beliefs using scientific methodology. It could be argued that the British Museum was the embodiment of this philosophy, representing the captivity and taming of ancient beliefs and knowledge.

Inscribed on the entablature above the south entrance to the King's Library is the quote 'The glory, jest and riddle of the world'. The line is from 'An Essay on Man' by Alexander Pope (1688–1744), an intense poem on the power struggle between Man and God. The context is that God's universe is an ordered structure, reflecting nature, balance and harmony, yet Man assumes it has been exclusively created for him and, using his newfound scientific knowledge, deigns to question its imperfect, convoluted, chaotic aspects. As such, Man is judging God.

Like Tennyson's aforementioned 'The Two Voices', the poem is suggestive of how little Man knows, despite the progress made by science. And Pope's message (as I see it) is that the quest for such knowledge is folly. Man has limited significance within the infinite scale of the divine creation. Instead, to lead a happy life, he should desist from challenging the 'Great Chain of Being', accept his position, and modestly strive for knowledge of himself; ours is not to reason why.

The justification of the Divine Order as a concept was, of course, examined in Milton's *Paradise Lost*, and Pope's idea of a 'stupendous whole' alludes to John Donne's 'Meditation XVII' ('No man is an island'). Mankind's hubristic convictions were also rejected by the subsequent Romantic and later existentialist movements.

The actual line 'The glory, jest and riddle of the world' refers to mankind. So, given the context of the poem, one may wonder why this particular citation was used above the portal to the Enlightenment room. It may be an ironic boastful celebration of the triumph of Man, the defeat of Mysticism and the victory of Science. Or perhaps, more generally, it represents the greatness, folly and inscrutability of the museum's cultural exhibits.

'An Essay on Man' comprised four epistles. Pope had intended to make it part of a larger work; however, he did not complete it. His contemporary, the French essayist Voltaire (1694–1778) once called 'An Essay on Man' the 'most beautiful, useful and sublime moral poem ever written in any language', but later went on to satirise such high-minded philosophy in his novel *Candide*.

POINT 4: CLYTIE BUST
(ROOM 1: KING'S LIBRARY)

Route: On entering King's Library from the Great Court, the bust is on the right.

William Wordsworth, 'The Egyptian Maid' (1828) (extracts)

While Merlin paced the Cornish sands,
Forth-looking toward the Rocks of Scilly,
The pleased Enchanter was aware
Of a bright Ship that seemed to hang in air,
Yet was she work of mortal hands,
And took from men her name – The Water Lily.

Soon did the gentle Nina reach
That Isle without a house or haven;
Landing, she found not what she sought,
Nor saw of wreck or ruin aught
But a carved Lotus cast upon the shore
By the fierce waves, a flower in marble graven.

Then Nina, stooping down, embraced,
With tenderness and mild emotion,
The Damsel, in that trance embound;
And, while she raised her from the ground,
And in the pearly shallop placed,
Sleep fell upon the air, and stilled the ocean.

'The tomb,' said Merlin, 'may not close
Upon her yet, earth hide her beauty;
Not froward to thy sovereign will
Esteem me, Liege! If I, whose skill
Wafted her hither, interpose
To check this pious haste of erring duty.

'For this, approaching, One by One,
Thy Knights must touch the cold hand of the Virgin;
So, for the favoured One, the Flower may bloom,
Once more; but, if unchangeable her doom,
If life departed be for ever gone,
Some blest assurance, from this cloud emerging.'

Then said Arthur, 'Take her to thy heart,
Sir Galahad! a treasure that God giveth,
Bound by indissoluble ties to thee,
Through mortal change and immortality;
Be happy and unenvied, thou who art
A goodly Knight that hath no Peer that liveth!'

The marble bust of 'Clytie' in the King's Library was acquired from Naples by antiquities collector Charles Townley (1737–1805) during a 1771 Grand Tour.

The sculpture is possibly of Roman origin, dating from around the year 50. The identity of the woman emerging from the leaves is much discussed. She was christened 'Clytie', after the character in Greek myth who was transformed into a sunflower after pining for the sun god Helios. However, some say she depicts Antonia, eldest daughter of the Roman general Mark Antony. Townley himself preferred that she represented the Egyptian earth goddess Isis.

The bust of Clytie was Townley's favourite object in his collection. He had it printed on his visiting card. When his house was under threat of burning down during the 1780 Gordon Riots, it was the one thing he said was worth rescuing, declaring, 'I must take care of my wife.' In Johan Zoffany's 1783 painting *The Townley Gallery*, the bust takes pride of place on the desk. The bust was eventually acquired by the museum.

The Clytie bust was influential in the art world, and many copies were sold. From 1855–1900, the Spode firm made copies in Parian ware. Minton produced similar models. It also inspired George Frederic Watts's first sculpture and Lord Frederic Leighton's last painting.

In the preface to his romantic poem of chivalry and conquest, 'An Egyptian Maid', William Wordsworth (1770–1850) notes that he was directly moved by the bust. The eponymous heroine (Wordsworth seems to agree with Townley on her origins) sails to Arthurian Britain but is shipwrecked when the suspicious wizard Merlin stirs up a tempest. Searching amongst the debris, Nina, the Lady of the Lake, finds the bust of a goddess appearing to rise out of a lotus. Then, finding the maid alive, Nina brings her to King Arthur's court, where she reveals that Arthur has freed Egypt from invaders. Alluring but pious, the maiden is then married to one of the most virtuous and chaste knights of the Round Table, Sir Galahad.

Certain political themes may be read into the poem, such as the justification of foreign military intervention, the folly of rationalism in the righteous crusade against tyranny, and, more generally, the immeasurable power of the female figure in a masculine world.

POINT 5: MAURICE'S INDIAN ANTIQUITIES
(ROOM 1: KING'S LIBRARY)

Route: In the King's Library, Indian Antiquities volumes are on the fourth shelf up in bookcase no. 188, on the opposite wall to the Great Court entrance.

Samuel Taylor Coleridge, 'Kubla Khan' (1816) (extracts)

In Xanadu did Kubla Khan
A stately pleasure-dome decree,
Where Alph the scared river ran,
Through caverns measureless to man,
Down to a sunless sea.

The shadow of the dome of pleasure
Floated midway on the waves;
Where was heard the mingled measure
From the fountain and the caves.
It was a miracle of rare device,
A sunny pleasure-dome with caves of ice!

Vicar, poet and noted oriental scholar Thomas Maurice (1754–1824) worked at the British Museum for most of his life. In 1799 he was appointed Assistant Librarian, and in 1810 Assistant Keeper of Manuscripts. Here he produced the seven-volume *Indian Antiquities* and the two-volume *History of Hindostan* as well as Indian-inspired poetry such as 'Hinda; an Eastern Elegy' (1779).

Maurice's poetry wasn't always well received. The Scottish poet Alexander Thomson wrote in 'The British Parnassus at the Close of the 18th Century' (1801), 'Maurice too must be mentioned, that resolute man, in tracing the Fables of old Hindostan; who contrives, though he can't Orientals peruse, to give to his song Orientalish hues.' Lady Anne Hamilton, daughter of the 9th Duke of Hamilton, mentions him in a satirical poem 'Epics of the Ton' (1807): 'Or warmed, like M-r-ce, by Museum fire, from Ganges dragged a hurdy-gurdy lyre.' And Lord Byron, in 'English Bards and Scotch Reviewers' (1809), wrote, 'So up thy hill, ambrosial Richmond! Heaves Dull Maurice all his granite weight of leaves . . .'

Despite the criticism of his poetry, Maurice's research of Indian mythology profoundly influenced the Romantic movement. Much inspired, Percy Bysshe Shelley set *Prometheus Unbound* in India, and Leigh Hunt, best remembered today for his exotically eastern 'Abou Ben Adhem', enjoyed many a chicken supper at the museum as a regular guest of his friend Maurice.

In 1797, Samuel Taylor Coleridge (1772–1834) was at the British Museum reading the *History of Hindostan* for use on a later project. In his notebook, he jotted down Maurice's memorable geographic descriptions of the Kashmir region:

In a cave in the mountains of Cashmere, two days before the new moon, there appears a bubble of ice which increases in size for 15 days, until it reaches quite a height. Then as the moon decreases, the image does also until it vanishes completely . . .

. . . her immediate utility in swelling the waters of that sacred river, whose annual inundations were the perpetual and abundant source of plenty . . .

. . . a trumpet, sounding from the king's pavilion, proclaimed the first appearance of the sun's beam, and that a golden image of its orb, enclosed in a circle of crystal, was then displayed in the front of that pavilion.

The lines helped to inspire one of the most famous poems of the Romantic period, 'Kubla Khan', which tells the story of the mythical summer palace of the thirteenth-century Mongol ruler and emperor of China. In the preface to his collection of poems, Coleridge claimed that the main idea for 'Kubla Khan' came to him after he awoke from a drug-induced dream, but the poem remained unfinished because he was interrupted. The poem was finally published in 1816 on the prompting of Lord Byron.

A number of other books in the museum library inspired Coleridge's 'fragmentary vision', such as the Marco Polo-inspired travelogue *Pilgrimes* (1613) by English clergyman and geographer Samuel Purchas:

In Xaindu did Cublai Can build a stately palace, encompassing sixteen miles of plaine ground with a wall, wherein are fertile meddowes, pleasant springs, delightful streams, and all sorts of beasts of chase and game, and in the middest thereof a sumptuous house of pleasure.

A manuscript copy of the poem in Coleridge's own handwriting was kept in the British Museum for many years. It can now be found amongst the Treasures of the British Library in St Pancras.

POINT 6: RAMESSES THE GREAT (ROOM 4: EGYPTIAN GALLERIES)

Route: From the King's Library, return to the Great Court and walk to the opposite side of the Reading Room. On entering Room 4, the Rosetta Stone display is facing you. The Ramesses statue is to the right of this display.

Percy Bysshe Shelley, 'Ozymandias' (1817)

I met a traveller from an antique land
Who said: 'Two vast and trunkless legs of stone
Stand in the desert. Near them, on the sand,
Half sunk, a shattered visage lies, whose frown,
And wrinkled lip, and sneer of cold command,
Tell that its sculptor well those passions read
Which yet survive, stamped on these lifeless things,
The hand that mocked them and the heart that fed:
And on the pedestal these words appear:
'My name is Ozymandias, king of kings:
Look on my works, ye Mighty, and despair!'
Nothing beside remains. Round the decay
Of that colossal wreck, boundless and bare
The lone and level sands stretch far away.'

Horace Smith, 'Ozymandias' (1817)

In Egypt's sandy silence, all alone,
Stands a gigantic Leg, which far off throws
The only shadow that the Desert knows: –
'I am great OZYMANDIAS,' saith the stone,
'The King of Kings; this mighty City shows
'The wonders of my hand.' – The City's gone, –
Nought but the Leg remaining to disclose
The site of this forgotten Babylon.
We wonder, – and some Hunter may express
Wonder like ours, when through the wilderness
Where London stood, holding the Wolf in chase,
He meets some fragment huge, and stops to guess
What powerful but unrecorded race
Once dwelt in that annihilated place.

The colossal statue of Ramesses II dominates the British Museum's Egyptian sculpture gallery. Ramesses, called the most powerful of the pharaohs, reigned from 1279 to 1212 BC, with the Egyptian empire reaching its greatest height under him. Worshipped as a god, he is said to have fathered over 150 children. He is the biblical figure of whom Moses demanded, 'Let my people go.'

Weighing over seven tons, his statue is carved from a single block of granite, the head being plain stone while the body is speckled. It features the standard pharaonic regalia of hat, beard and cobra diadem. It was originally one of a pair seated at the entrance to a royal tomb in Thebes. At some point, the head and upper torso of the statue fell into the sand near the complex.

The hole in the chest was made during an unsuccessful attempt by French archaeologists to remove the statue in 1798; the same expedition saw the acquisition of the Rosetta Stone. The Italian explorer Giovanni Belzoni was commissioned by British authorities to remove the statue in a project begun in 1816. It took seventeen days and 130 men to tow it to the Nile ready for shipment to London, where it finally arrived in 1818. Known on arrival as the Younger Memnon, it went on display in the British Museum later that year and was the first Egyptian sculpture recognised as a work of art by western scholars.

Almost 2,000 years earlier, the Greek historian Siculus came across a similar statue at Thebes and noted an inscription on it: 'I am Ozymandias, King of Kings. If anyone would know how great I am and where I lie, let him dare to surpass my achievements.' (Ozymandias was an alternate name for the pharaoh.)

In 1817, the Romantic poet Percy Bysshe Shelley (1792–1822) and his stockbroker friend Horace Smith (1779–1849) challenged each other to write a poem anticipating the arrival of the Younger Memnon to Britain. Both were entitled 'Ozymandias'. The next month, Leigh Hunt's cultural periodical *The Examiner* printed Shelley's poem, with Smith's version in a subsequent issue. Neither had seen the actual statue, although it is likely detailed sketches were available, such was the excitement of its imminent display and of general Egyptomania at the time. 'Ozymandias' is one of Shelley's most famous works alongside *Prometheus Unbound*.

Some mocked the clumsiness of Smith's amateur version compared to Shelley's intuitive dexterity. However, if Shelley's skilfully delivered message is 'all glory is fleeting', Smith's saving grace may be in the prescience of his second stanza, in which he imagines the future ruins of imperial Britain, and muses on whether a similar fragmentary object might also inspire such wonder.

POINT 7: MAUSOLUS AND ARTEMISIA (ROOM 21: HALICARNASSUS)

Route: Pass through Room 4 (behind Ramesses) to West Stairs landing. Take steps down to right of stairwell. Go through doors and take steps up into Room 21.

W B Yeats, 'He Wishes for the Cloths of Heaven' (1899)

Had I the heavens' embroidered cloths,
Enwrought with golden and silver light,
The blue and the dim and the dark cloths
Of night and light and the half-light,
I would spread the cloths under your feet:
But I, being poor, have only my dreams;
I have spread my dreams under your feet;
Tread softly because you tread on my dreams.

In modern-day Turkey lie the ruins of the great Mausoleum of Halicarnassus. It was built around 350 BC and feted as one of the seven wonders of the ancient world. Along the top were placed 750 brightly painted statues depicting chariot groups, hunting scenes and dynastic portraits. Prominent were two marble statues that experts maintain are part of a family tree. Tradition has it they depict King Mausolus, governor of the Greek province of Charia (Halicarnassus), and his queen (and sister) Artemisia, who had the tomb built on his death. The word *mausoleum* derives from it.

The first-century Roman writer Pliny the Elder noted the original dimensions: about 410ft in perimeter on a north-south axis by 140ft high, with thirty-six columns supporting a twenty-four-step pyramid.

The Mausoleum remained structurally intact until a thirteenth-century earthquake. In the sixteenth century, the Knights Hospitaller used some of the ruined stone to build St Peter's Castle in Bodrum. In 1846, Stratford Canning, the British ambassador to Constantinople, was given permission by the sultan to remove the sculptures and take them back to London. Ten years later, Charles Newton, British Museum curator of Greek antiquities, excavated the rest of the site, and a number of sculptures from the original structure, including 'Mausolus' and 'Artemisia', arrived at the museum.

The Irish playwright and poet laureate W B Yeats (1865–1939) often visited the museum's galleries and was much influenced by the various classical sculptures. When describing the British writer and impresario Florence Farr, known as the 'bohemian's bohemian', Yeats said she had 'a tranquil beauty like that of Demeter's image near the British Museum Reading Room door'. On his contemporary, the poet Lionel Johnson, he wrote, 'He had the delicate strong features of a certain filleted head of a Greek athlete in the British Museum ...'

The Mausolus and Artemisia statues commanded special attention from Yeats. They seemed to symbolise the uncontrived enthusiasm of an artist. He constantly refers to them in his memoirs, *The Trembling of the Veil* (1922):

I thought constantly of Homer and Dante, and the tombs of Mausolus and Artemisia, the great figures of King and Queen ...

I had gone a great distance from my first poems, from all that I had copied from the folk-art of Ireland, as from the statue of Mausolus and his Queen ...

Morris set out to make a revolution that the persons of his Well at the World's End or his Waters of the Wondrous Isles, always, to my mind, in the likeness of Artemisia and her man, might walk his native scenery ...

The statues of Mausolus and Artemisia at the British Museum, private, half-animal, half-divine figures, all unlike the Grecian athletes and Egyptian kings in their near neighbourhood ...

The statue of Artemisia, in particular, reminded Yeats of Maud Gonne, the Irish revolutionary he'd met in 1889 and with whom he had become obsessed. He suggested a Greek sculptor would find Gonne the very model of beauty:

Her whole body seemed a masterwork of long labouring thought, as though a Scopas had measured and calculated, consorted with Egyptian sages, and mathematicians out of Babylon, that he might outface even Artemisia's sepulchral image with a living norm.

Yeats dedicated a number of poems inspired by the statues to Maud Gonne, including his famous 'He Wishes for the Cloths of Heaven'.

POINT 8: CARYATID
(ROOM 19: GREEK GALLERIES)

Route: From Room 21, go through the entrance to Room 20 (to the right when facing the statues of Mausolus and Artemisia). Pass through into Room 19. As you exit Room 19, the caryatid is on the right.

Dollie Radford, 'To the Caryatid (in the Elgin Room)' (1895)

So long ago, and day by day,
I came to learn from you, to pray,
You did not hear, you did not know
The thing I craved, so long ago.

The days were always days of spring,
Hope laid her hand on everything,
And in your spacious room, on me,
She rested it most lovingly.

Of all the season's sun and showers,
I gathered up the fairest flowers,
And brought my garlands, fresh and sweet,
To place in gladness at your feet

And prayed to stand in strength, as you
Through the long years untried and new
With dauntless mien and steadfast gaze,
To bear the burden of the days.

Now many tired years are told,
My prayer long since is dead and cold,
You were too wise to grant it me,
Although I prayed so patiently.

But at your feet my flowers lie,
The happy flowers which cannot die,
I see them through my tears, and know
They are as sweet as long ago.

Displayed in the Greek sculpture galleries is a statue of a female figure used as a supporting column and known as a *caryatid*. About eight feet tall and carved from Pentelic marble, she was originally one of six sculpted for the roof of the Erechtheum, the temple which stands alongside the Parthenon on the Acropolis in Athens. On her head, it appears that she wears a crown, but it is in fact a decorated architectural capital that supports the roof above.

Caryatids are also represented on the eastern section of the Parthenon frieze in the museum. They are so named after the maidens of the ancient Greek town of Caryae, who danced while balancing baskets on their heads.

The Erechtheum was completed a few decades after the Parthenon, in about 415 BC. The caryatid's five 'sisters' remain in Athens, but this one became part of the British Museum's collection via Lord Elgin.

Exactly 1,000 yards north of the museum stands St Pancras New Church, designed by William Inwood and completed in 1822. Flanking each side of the church are four caryatids based on those from the Erechtheum.

The radical English poet Dollie Radford (1858–1920) wrote a verse on the feminine strength symbolically represented by the caryatid. Radford, née Maitland, met her poet husband Ernest at the museum. This poem reflects the years of caring for her husband while he suffered from mental illness.

POINT 9: PARTHENON SCULPTURES (ROOM 18: DUVEEN GALLERY)

Route: From Room 19, go through Room 17 (Nereid monument). Turn right into Room 18 (Duveen Gallery). The Parthenon sculptures adorn the room.

Lord Byron, 'Childe Harold's Pilgrimage' (1812–18) (extract)

Dull is the eye that will not weep to see
Thy walls defaced, thy mouldering shrines removed
By British hands, which it had best behoved
To guard those relics ne'er to be restored.

Lord Byron, 'The Curse of Minerva' (1811) (extracts)

Seekest thou the cause of loathing? Look around.
Escaped from the ravage of the Turk and Goth,
Thy country sends a spoiler worse than both.
That all may learn from whence the plunderer came,
The insulted wall sustains his hated name:
For Elgin's fame thus grateful Pallas pleads,
Below, his name – above, behold his deeds!
Yet still the gods are just, and crimes are crossed:
See here what Elgin won, and what he lost!
Some calm spectator, as he takes his view,
In silent indignation mixed with grief,
Admires the plunder, but abhors the thief.

Felicia Hemans, 'Modern Greece' (1817) (extracts)

Oh! who hath trod thy consecrated clime,
Fair land of Phidias! theme of lofty strains!
And traced each scene, that, 'midst the wrecks of time,
The print of Glory's parting step retains;

But thou, fair world! Whose fresh unsullied charms
Welcomed Columbus from the western wave,
Wilt thou receive the wanderer to thine arms,
The lost descendant of the immortal brave?

Glory to those whose relics thus arrest
The gaze of ages! Glory to the free!
For they, they only, could have thus impressed
Their mighty image on the years to be!

Their glance is cold indifference, and their toil
But to destroy what ages have revered,
As if exulting sternly to erase
Whatever might prove that land had nursed a nobler race.

And who may grieve that, rescued from their hands,
Spoilers of excellence and foes to art,
Thy relics, Athens! Borne to other lands,
Claim homage still to thee from every heart?

Yet art thou honoured in each fragment still
That wasting years and barbarous hands had spared;
Each hallowed stone, from rapine's fury borne,
Shall wake right dreams of thee in ages yet unborn.

Mark – on the storied frieze the graceful train,
The holy festival's triumphal throng,
In fair procession, to Minerva's fane,
With many a sacred symbol, move along.

There every shade of bright existence trace,
The fire of youth, the dignity of age;
The matron's calm austerity of grace,
The ardent warrior, the benignant sage;

And who can tell how pure, how bright a flame,
Caught from these models, may illume the west?
What British Angelo may rise to fame,
On the free isle what beams of art may rest?

Nations unborn shall track thine own blue deep,
To hail thy shore, to worship thy remains;
Thy mighty monuments with reverence trace,
And cry, 'This ancient soil hath nursed a glorious race!'

One of the most influential buildings in the world, the Parthenon was completed in 432 BC on the Acropolis in Athens. The classic design inspired architecture of the Roman empire, the Renaissance and the Enlightenment.

The Parthenon, or 'Room of Maidens', was built after a series of Greek victories over the Persians and other city-states, replacing a temple destroyed in the Greco-Persian war. It was dedicated to Athena (Minerva), the goddess of the city. The structure was 200ft long, 100ft wide and 64ft high. Forty-six columns and two pediments supported the roof. Twenty thousand tons of marble were used. The design is attributed to Phidias, who was also responsible for the statue of Zeus at Olympia. There were two rooms: one a temple, the other a treasury. Stored in this strongroom was the protection money from other Greek city-states extracted in return for the defence against the Persians.

On the inside and outside walls, friezes and metopes were decorated with sculptures. These were sculpted directly out of the structural marble, not added on. They have an overlapping 3D effect, with defined, detailed and realistic anatomy.

The sculptures represent the birth of western art history and the basis for our dominant visual culture. Endowed with consciousness, they tell a story through expressions and emotions. The ancient Greeks depicted contemporary ordinary people heroically. Their sculpture remained pretty much unequalled until the Renaissance began 1,500 years later.

The sculptures for the pediments (the triangular structures that supported the pitched roof) told stories from the canon of Greek myth. The west pediment depicts Athena's victory over Poseidon for Attica. The east pediment depicted the birth of Athena from the head of Zeus with Hercules, Dionysus, Demeter, Persephone, Zeus's servant Hebe, Hestia and possibly Aphrodite in attendance. The final figure in the pantheon is a horse head representing Selene, the moon goddess. Sinking after a day's ride with bulging eyes and flared nostrils, it is one of the most iconic images of western art.

We have a good description of the frieze sculptures from a guidebook of 150 AD by the Roman writer Pausanias. The sculptures depict the Pan Athenian (a four-yearly festival dedicated to the goddess Athena, celebrated by the ten tribes of Athens) and a royal scene showing the Olympian gods: Zeus, bearded and enthroned; Hera, his wife; Dionysus, the god of wine; Demeter, the goddess of fertility (pining for her daughter Persephone carried off by Hades); Ares, the god of war, and Hermes, the messenger god with staff and hat.

The museum friezes are at present displayed at eye level. This offers an odd perspective, as they were meant to be seen from forty feet below. It should also be noted that the original building and its statues were painted quite garishly. This is important because 'classicism' is often guided by aesthetic notions based on pure white marble sculpture.

The British Museum collection also contains fifteen of the original ninety-two metope sculptures. These are in high relief – as close to statues as possible without being free-standing. The metopes depict mythical battle scenes, including the fight between the Lapiths and centaurs at Hippodamia's wedding.

It is a minor miracle any remains of the Parthenon have survived at all. Around 200 BC, the statue of Athena was destroyed by fire. In 400 AD, the Christians damaged pagan images while converting to a church. In

1458, the Ottoman Turks captured the church and converted it to a mosque. They later used the treasury to store gunpowder. In 1687, the Venetians attacked with cannon and blew up the gunpowder store. The Venetians tried to take the statues from the pediments, but the ropes broke and much damage was done. Sometime in the 1700s, the Turks built a smaller mosque in the centre of the building and left the rest to ruin.

In 1799, Lord Elgin, army officer and ambassador to the Ottoman empire, paid £25,000 of his own cash for a team to make 10,000 drawings and plaster casts of the Parthenon; these are still used for restoration today. Two years later, as a diplomatic gift, Elgin's team was allowed to buy and remove around 40% of the frieze that interested them. But it proved an expensive salvage operation that lasted several years, and Elgin borrowed £70,000 to remove the marbles. It was also a somewhat bungled excavation. To make matters worse, a ship sank with some stones on board. Elgin then borrowed the money to build a museum to exhibit the marbles. In 1816, he tried to get his money back from Parliament, who challenged him as to whether the marbles were legally his. He was eventually forced to sell them at half the price he paid and they were passed to the British Museum. In 1841, Elgin died in Paris owing £150,000.

But the trials and tribulations of the Parthenon and its sculptures do not end there. In the 1920s, a disastrous rebuild of the temple at the original site was undertaken by the architect Balanos, and since 1986 the Greeks have been trying to rectify the damage with a restoration. In 1938, the art collector Lord Duveen financed a purpose-built gallery to house the sculptures in the British Museum. He also paid for them to be cleaned, and they were, far too aggressively. They then spent World War II in storage at Aldwych underground station. It was just as well. The Duveen Gallery was hit four times by bombs during World War II and did not properly open until 1962.

The Parthenon sculptures have inspired some of the most passionate poems in the English language. Lord Byron (1788–1824) reacted with fury in 1809 when Elgin's agent gave him a tour of the Parthenon with the now-missing sculptures. Byron was a bitter opponent of their removal and denounced Elgin's actions in his poems 'The Curse of Minerva' and 'Childe Harold's Pilgrimage', which contended that the faults were manifold: the treasures were forcibly stolen, the grandeur of the original location left vandalised, the artefacts were unappreciated by their new hosts, and the country bore shame. The debate had nothing to do with politics, value or merit. Neither the Parthenon nor its marbles are described in the poems. It is a battle between idealistic romanticism and pragmatic rationalism.

'Modern Greece' by Felicia Hemans (1793–1835) is based on the British Government Select Committee's conclusions on keeping the collection at the British Museum. While lamenting lost ancient cultures such as those of Arabia, Byzantium and Greece, she makes no apologies for the removal of the marbles and, in a subtle dig at Byron, paints a vivid description of them. Her title alone riled Byron, who wrote, 'Why "*modern?*" You may say *modern Greeks*, but surely *Greece* itself is rather more ancient than ever it was.'

Perhaps what Hemans was getting at was that the glory of modern Britain is manifest in the exhibition of the ancient world. She had already made the point, in 'The Restoration of the Works of Art to Italy' (1816), that, although Rome physically conquered Jerusalem, it was Jerusalem that spiritually conquered Rome. Here, she was asking if modern Britain had not raped Greece, but had, in effect, been seduced by her.

POINT 10: KEATS ON THE PARTHENON SCULPTURES (DUVEEN GALLERY)

Route: In the Duveen Gallery (Room 18), the 'Keats lowing heifer' is on the opposite wall on entering Room 18 (south frieze panels 132–136).

John Keats, 'On Seeing the Elgin Marbles' (1817) (extract)

Haydon! forgive me that I cannot speak
Definitively of these mighty things;
Forgive me, that I have not eagle's wings,
That what I want I know not where to seek,
And think that I would not be over-meek,
In rolling out upfollowed thunderings,
Even to the steep of Heliconian springs,
Were I of ample strength for such a freak.
Think, too, that all these numbers should be thine;
Whose else? In this who touch thy vesture's hem?
For, when men stared at what was most divine
With brainless idiotism and overwise phlegm,
Thou hadst beheld the full Hesperian shine
Of their star in the east, and gone to worship them.

John Keats, 'Sonnet on the Elgin Marbles' (1817) (extracts)

My spirit is too weak – mortality
Weighs heavily on me like unwilling sleep
And each imagined pinnacle and steep
Of godlike hardship tells me I must die
Like a sick Eagle looking at the sky.
Yet 'tis a gentle luxury to weep
That I have not the cloudy winds to sweep
Fresh for the opening of the morning's eye.

Such dim-conceived glories of the brain
Bring round the heart an indescribable feud;
So do these wonders a most dizzy pain,
Which mingles Grecian grandeur with the rude
Wasting of old Time – with a billowy main –
A sun – a shadow of a magnitude.

John Keats, 'Ode on a Grecian Urn' (1819) (extract)

Who are these coming to the sacrifice?
To what green altar, O mysterious priest,
Leadest thou that heifer lowing at the skies,
And all her silken flanks with garlands drest?

Two poems on the Parthenon sculptures by John Keats (1795–1821) appeared in the *Examiner* periodical in 1817. One was written in reply to his friend, the painter Ben Haydon, who, like Hemans, had championed the sculptures as a work of art. Keats noted:

> *In regard to this subject it will be remembered that Haydon had been most energetic in preaching the gospel of the Elgin Marbles, and that his friends claimed for him the distinction of being the first to apply to modern art the 'principles' of those immortal works.*

The second poem, 'Sonnet on the Elgin Marbles', shows that Keats, on the one hand, celebrates the awe induced by viewing the sculptures, but, on the other, remains troubled by them.

It is also claimed that a section of the Parthenon frieze was a direct inspiration for lines in Keats's classic 'Ode on a Grecian Urn'. The panel in question shows a heifer lowing as it is led to be sacrificed at the altar of Athena.

POINT 11: ASSYRIAN BULLS
(ROOM 10: ASSYRIAN GALLERIES)

Route: From the Duveen Gallery (Room 18), return to Room 17 and
pass through into Room 23. Turn right. Bulls are facing you
in Room 10.

D G Rossetti, 'The Burden of Nineveh'
(1856, revised 1869) (extracts)

Sighing, I turned at last to win
Once more the London dirt and din;
And as I made the swing-door spin
And issued, they were hoisting in
A wing-èd beast from Nineveh.

A human face the creature wore,
And hoofs behind, and hoofs before,
And flanks with dark runes fretted o'er.
'Twas bull, 'twas mitred Minotaur,
The very corpse of Nineveh.

What vows, what rites, what prayers preferred,
What songs has the strange image heard?
In what blind vigil stood interred
For ages, till an English word
Broke silence first at Nineveh?

'While school-foundations in the act
Of holiday, three files compact,
Shall learn to view thee as a fact.
Connected with that zealous tract:
Rome – Babylon and Nineveh.'

'Greece, Egypt, Rome, did any god
Before whose feet men knelt unshod
Deem that in this unblessed abode
Another scarce more unknown god
Should house with him, from Nineveh?'

'And now – they and their gods and thou
All relics here together – now . . .'
Whose profit? Whether bull or cow,
Isis or Ibis, who or how,
Whether of Thebes or Nineveh?

So may he stand again; till now,
In ships of unknown sail and prow,
Some tribe of the Australian plough
Bear him afar, – a relic now
Of London, not of Nineveh!

The Assyrian Bulls are the largest objects in the British Museum. At over fourteen feet tall, the two sixteen-ton blocks of gypsum are about 2,700 years old.

Originally brightly painted, they once straddled a gateway in the citadel of Khorsabad, the palace of the biblical king Sargon II, who reigned from 721 to 705 BC. Also known as *lamassu*, an Assyrian protective deity, they are possibly symbolic of royal virtues: the head, wisdom of man; the wings, speed of an eagle; the body, strength of a bull. Similar figures from the Palace of Nimrud feature a lion's body, perhaps representing courage.

Behind each bull is a winged angel-like figure, possibly a priest in holy ritual. He has dipped a pine cone or sponge into an anointing oil and is sprinkling it over the animal. While the bulls are a mirror image of each other, the holy men are not, as both are using the sacred right hand.

It may be noted that such symbolism found its way into the Christian sphere. The evangelists Matthew, Mark, Luke and John were represented by an angel, lion, bull and eagle respectively. Such a tetramorphic beast is also depicted in the mosaic pavement at St Thomas Beckett's shrine in Canterbury Cathedral. One is also reminded of Alexander Pope's aforementioned 'Essay on Man':

> *What would this man? Now upward will he soar,*
> *And little less than angel, would be more;*
> *Now looking downwards, just as grieved appears*
> *To want the strength of bulls, and the fur of bears.*
> *Made for his use, all creatures if he call,*
> *Say what their use, had he the powers of all.*

After an initial expansion around Mesopotamia from 1100 to 1000 BC, the Assyrian empire saw several rises and falls. From 721 to 650 BC, under consecutive rulers Sargon, Sennacherib and Ashurbanipal, it controlled the entire Middle East from modern-day Iran to the Mediterranean. Civil war brought a final decline.

The Palace of Khorsabad was rediscovered in 1842 by French archaeologist Paul-Émile Botta. In 1849, Henry Rawlinson, a British diplomat in Baghdad, bought the bulls from the French Consul and had them each sawn into four pieces (quite brutally, it appears), then shipped to the British Museum.

'The Burden of Nineveh' by Dante Gabriel Rossetti (1828–1882) marks the arrival of the Assyrian Bulls to the British Museum in 1852, and in some ways mirrors Byron's take on the Parthenon sculptures. The poem suggests that artefacts are demystified and compete for attention when crudely exhibited in incongruous juxtaposition. The poem also predicts that one day, modern artefacts will compete with ancient ones, and ponders a future civilisation, perhaps Australian, plundering the ruins of the British empire and presuming the Assyrian Bull is actually a relic of London rather than Nineveh.

POINT 12: ANTINOUS AS BACCHUS (ROOM 70, UPPER FLOOR)

Route: Pass through Assyrian galleries (Rooms 10, 7 and 6). At the end of Room 6, turn left and pass through the south cloakroom and shop to the main foyer. Turn sharply left and go up the South Stairs. At the top of the stairs, turn sharply right and pass through Rooms 68 and 69 into Room 70. The bust is on a plinth on the right, near the centre of the room.

Edward Dowden, 'Antinous Crowned as Bacchus (In the British Museum)' (1876)

Who crowned thy forehead with the ivy-wreath
And clustered berries burdening the hair?
Who gave thee godhood, and dim rites? Beware
O beautiful, who breathest mortal breath.
Thou delicate flame great gloom environeth!
The gods are free, and drink a stainless air,
And lightly on calm shoulders they upbear
A weight of joy eternal, nor can Death
Cast o'er their sleep the shadow of her shrine.
O thou confessed too mortal by the over-fraught
Crowned forehead, must thy drooped eyes ever see
The glut of pleasure, those pale lips of thine
Still suck a bitter-sweet satiety,
Thy soul descend through cloudy realms of thought?

Antinous was the favourite youth of the Roman emperor Hadrian. A bust in Room 70 of the British Museum is said to depict him in the character of Bacchus, god of wine and revelry, crowned with a wreath of ivy.

The bust was found in 1770 near the Villa Pamphili in Rome. The British collector Charles Townley acquired it and it later passed to the museum. The Irish poet Edward Dowden (1843–1913) wrote a verse on the exhibit in 1876.

POINT 13: PORTLAND VASE
(ROOM 70: UPPER FLOOR)

Route: In Room 70, the vase is in a glass display case on the right in the centre of the room as you go towards Room 71.

Erasmus Darwin, 'The Botanic Garden' (1791) (extract)

Over the fine forms of Portland's mystic urn,
Here by the fallen columns and disjoined arcades,
On mouldering stones beneath deciduous shades,
Sits humankind in hieroglyphic state.

John Keats, 'Ode on a Grecian Urn' (1819)

Thou still unravish'd bride of quietness,
Thou foster-child of silence and slow time,
Sylvan historian, who canst thus express
A flowery tale more sweetly than our rhyme:
What leaf-fringed legend haunts about thy shape,
Of deities or mortals, or of both?
What men or gods are these? What maidens loath?
What mad pursuit? What struggle to escape?
What pipes and timbrels? What wild ecstasy?

Heard melodies are sweet, but those unheard
Are sweeter; therefore, ye soft pipes, play on;
Not to the sensual ear, but, more endear'd,
Pipe to the spirit ditties of no tone:
Fair youth, beneath the trees, thou canst not leave
Thy song, nor ever can those trees be bare;
Bold Lover, never, never canst thou kiss,
Though winning near the goal yet, do not grieve;
She cannot fade, though thou hast not thy bliss,
Forever wilt thou love, and she be fair!

Ah, happy, happy boughs! that cannot shed
Your leaves, nor ever bid the Spring adieu;
And, happy melodist, unwearied,
Forever piping songs for ever new;
More happy love! more happy, happy love!
Forever warm and still to be enjoy'd,
Forever panting, and forever young;
All breathing human passion far above,
That leaves a heart high-sorrowful and cloy'd,
A burning forehead, and a parching tongue.

Who are these coming to the sacrifice?
To what green altar, O mysterious priest,
Leadest thou that heifer lowing at the skies,
And all her silken flanks with garlands drest?
What little town by river or sea shore,
Or mountain-built with peaceful citadel,
Is emptied of this folk, this pious morn?

And, little town, thy streets for evermore
Will silent be; and not a soul to tell
Why thou art desolate, can e'er return.

O Attic shape! Fair attitude! with brede
Of marble men and maidens overwrought,
With forest branches and the trodden weed;
Thou, silent form, dost tease us out of thought,
As doth eternity: Cold Pastoral!
When old age shall this generation waste,
Thou shalt remain, in midst of other woe
Than ours, a friend to man, to whom thou say'st,
'Beauty is truth, truth beauty – that is all
Ye know on earth, and all ye need to know.'

The Portland vase, in Room 70, is one of the world's oldest and most famous pieces of blown glassware. Reputed to be over 2,000 years old, it was the inspiration for many pottery techniques and styles, especially those of Wedgwood and Minton.

The production of blown glass involves the base material silicon (sand) being melted at high temperatures to allow it to recrystallise. As it cools it can be formed into shapes using a blowpipe. The vase was coloured blue by adding cobalt. A raised relief design or 'cameo' was applied by dipping it into melted white glass, which was then etched by a skilled engraver.

The design on the vase is one of the great mysteries of its provenance. Is it depicting a classical myth? Orpheus and Eurydice? Peleus and Thetis? Apollo and Augustus? Antony and Cleopatra? An allegory of life and death? There are many other mysteries concerning the vase over its 2,000-year history, and it is difficult to say whether it has led a charmed life or a cursed one.

Erasmus Darwin (1731–1802), physician, botanist and poet, and grandfather of the naturalist Charles, wrote a direct homage to the vase after his friend Josiah Wedgwood sent him a copy of it. Darwin explained his interpretation of the vase's decoration as an allegory of man's passage from life to death.

The poem was illustrated with plates by William Blake and published in part in 1791. It was a hit amongst the Romantics, admired by both Coleridge and Wordsworth, and, as a result of such attention, the vase became stamped on the national psyche.

John Keats's 'Ode on a Grecian Urn' does not directly refer to a single urn. In fact, no exact combination of the figures and scenes he described has ever been found, and it is unlikely that one was known to Keats. However, we do know that Keats visited an exhibition of Greek artefacts accompanying the Parthenon sculptures at the British Museum, and many scholars believe that Keats had a composite of exhibits in mind, suggesting that it may be in equal parts Portland vase, Townley vase, Sosibios vase and Parthenon frieze.

The second-century Townley vase, found near Rome, was bought in 1774 by the British collector Charles Townley. The vase had been reconstructed and was decorated in high relief with a musical scene featuring the deity Pan and the wild followers of Bacchus. A similar theme is on the Sosibios vase in the Louvre, a sketch of which is attributed to Keats. As previously mentioned, a section of the Parthenon frieze depicts an aspect of the Panathenaic festival where cattle and sheep were led to be sacrificed at the great altar of Athena. One panel shows a heifer lowing before the slaughter, and a caption below it suggests it was the inspiration for those respective lines in the Ode. It is the last verse, however, that lends itself to the Portland vase, as Keats's description of overwrought figures encourages some to believe them standing against a darker background. Thus the poem is indirectly ekphrastic, as it does not describe a particular object so much as create an image in readers' minds.

Timeline of the Portland Vase

c.25BC–25AD: Created, possibly in Phoenicia (Lebanon) – the world's biggest producers of blown glass at the time – and sold to the Roman market.

1582:   Taken from tomb of third-century Roman emperor Severus II. Sold privately.

1600:   Subject of correspondence for artists Caravaggio and Rubens.

1601–1778:   Owned by Cardinal del Monte, Pope Urban VIII of the Barberini family. In Italy, it is still sometimes known as the Barberini vase.

1778:   Sold to British Ambassador to Naples William Hamilton.

1784:   Sold to Dowager Duchess of Portland, who obsessively hid it from view.

1786:   Inherited by 3rd Duke of Portland (a future Prime Minister).

1789:   Wedgwood made copy in Jasperware and adopted image as his logo.

1809:   3rd Duke of Portland died. 4th Duke loaned the vase to British Museum.

1845:   Broken into 150 pieces when a visitor to the museum hurled a rock at it. As there was no law against destroying antiquities, the man was fined just £3 for disorderly conduct. The Duke of Portland paid the fine. The vase was glued back together, although over thirty fragments were lost for the next hundred years.

1945:   Portland family sold to British Museum. The vase underwent further repair.

1989:   British Museum experts purposely broke the vase again, then restored it using modern methods. They also inserted the chips left over after the original repair. The vase has been repaired three times overall to fix the damage.

POINT 14: MUMMY OF ARTEMIDORUS (ROOM 62: UPPER FLOOR)

Route: Pass through Rooms 71, 72, 73, and upper landing into room 61. Turn right and into Room 62. Mummy is in glass display case on the left in centre of room.

Edward Carpenter, 'Artemidorus, Farewell' (1896) (extracts)

Could I but see thee once, or hope to see –
One hair of thy head, one finger of thy hand,
To hear one little word more from thy lips –
'Twere more than all the world. But now the priests
Have got thee in their clutches; and already
They wrap the sacred linen o'er thy head,
Thy features and thy hair they cover up,
And round thy arms thy fingers and thy hands
They wind and wind and wind and wind the bands,
And I shall see thee nevermore, my own.
And then they'll paint
Thy likeness on the outer mummy case,
And stand it by the wall, as if to mock me,
Throwing my arms around a lifeless shell,
Breaking my heart against it.

And in a hundred years stray folk will come
And ask, 'Who was Artemidorus pray?'
Nor listen for an answer – if in sooth
There's any that can give one. And in time
Strangers perhaps will overrun our land
And violate thy coffin, and unbind
With sacrilegious hands the rags, and find
Only a little dust – Ah! nothing else ...

Artemidorus dear,
Dearest of all things either in earth or heaven,
For the long silence but one word remains,
Remains but this – 'Farewell.'

The Egyptian galleries on the upper floor of the British Museum contain the most sought-after exhibits for visitors: mummies.

Mummy derives from the Arabic *mummia*, the word for a substance similar to tar. The ancient Egyptian mummification process involved the complete artificial preservation of the body at a house of beautification. The technique was perfected about 2600 BC, roughly parallel with the building of the early pyramids.

The ritualistic procedure involved the removal of internal organs, which slowed decomposition. An incision was made on the left-hand side of the body to remove the stomach, intestines, lungs and liver. These were dried, embalmed, wrapped and placed in four stone 'canopic' jars. The heart and kidneys were taken out and dried. The chest and abdomen were then rinsed out with wine and spices and the heart and kidneys put back in. The brain was pulled out via the nostril. The skull was then filled with sawdust. The body cavities were packed with linen bags filled with natron and salt crystals. The incision was stitched up; the skin washed and massaged with oils and spices to restore suppleness. The body was covered with a mixture of tar, natron, spices and resins and left for seventy days to complete the embalming process. Then the body was wrapped in bandages. Up to 450 square yards of linen were used. This took a further fifteen days. The linen was stiffened with plaster. In all, the whole treatment took about three months.

Some coffins featured a portrait of the inhabitant. One such example in the British Museum collection inspired a poem by the English philosopher-poet Edward Carpenter (1844–1929). He wrote an ode to a Greek youth whose portrait was painted on a wooden panel. A Greek inscription tells us that the youth was named Artemidorus.

At a cost of around £50,000, only the wealthy ruling class could afford mummification. It continued as a funerary process in various cultures in Europe over the centuries, in particular in Greece and Italy. Indeed, a version of mummification was still being practised in Sicily well into the twentieth century.

POINT 15: FLOOD TABLET
(ROOM 55: UPPER FLOOR)

Route: From Room 62, pass through into Room 63. Turn right into
Room 56. Turn left and pass through into Room 55. The tablet is in a
glass display case on the right at the end of the room.

Anon, Epic of Gilgamesh (translated extracts)

*Utnapishtim spoke: 'One night I had a dream that the gods were secretly
planning to send a great flood to wipe out mankind.*

*'A voice told me to tear down my house and build a boat. I was given precise
measurements, and orders that on this boat I was to take my family and a
male and female of every species of animal.*

*'Then the great deluge was sent and continued for many days. Finally, the
waters subsided. The boat came to rest on a mountain top.
I set free a bird that did not return and I knew there was dry land.*

*'The gods were furious that I had discovered their secret plans.
They did not want man to survive, so they made me a god too.'*

If you visit the British Museum with the above poems in hand, I hope you will enjoy looking at the exhibits in a new dimension. But, before you finish your tour, take the opportunity to view the oldest poem known to mankind.

It is found on the Flood Tablet, which just happens to be an exhibit in itself, and can be found in the Assyrian galleries on the upper floor.

In 1878, the Syrian archaeologist Hormuzd Rassam made an incredible discovery while excavating the 2,600-year-old Nineveh Palace of Ashurbanipal in modern-day Iraq. Amongst the ancient ruins of the library, he came across some clay tablets carved in cuneiform, the Assyrian wedge-shaped writing system.

One contained the world's oldest known work of literature, the *Epic of Gilgamesh*. This 5,000-year-old poem was well-known in antiquity, influencing heroic epics such as Homer's *Iliad* and *Odyssey*. The poem is incomplete; fragments were still being discovered in the twenty-first century. But we do have the general gist of the story: the Babylonian king Gilgamesh begins a quest for knowledge and immortality. He meets his grandfather Utnapishtim and asks him how he has achieved eternal life. Utnapishtim reveals he had been made a deity after he had discovered the gods' secret plan to send a mighty flood to wipe out mankind.

When the fragments were deciphered, they created a world sensation, as they revealed an interpretation of the Noah's Ark story, but one *older* than the Bible version. Other cultural versions of the flood story are also known; one is depicted in a Roman mosaic in the British Museum. Many experts think that the biblical flood may have been the result of a tsunami caused by an earthquake or meteor.

POINT 16: POSTSCRIPT: ART VERSUS ART (PEDIMENT)

Route (exit): Pass through Room 54 and take East Stairs down to ground level. Turn left and pass through Room 4 (King's Library). Turn right for Great Court and the exit. The pediment is above the main entrance outside.

Whether or not a poet of the British empire had personal misgivings on the morality of museums, they certainly indulged themselves in reinterpreting the visual objects into dramatic verbal descriptions. In some cases, the poems themselves are elevated to a higher aesthetic plane than the original artefact; Shelley's 'Ozymandias' may be the most obvious case in point. Thus we might well ask a consequential question: do words have more durability than objects?

Yes, argues 'dreamer of dreams' Arthur O'Shaughnessy in his 'Ode' (1873): 'Yet we are the movers and shakers of the world for ever, it seems. With wonderful deathless ditties ...' Or the little-known seventeenth-century English bard Leonard Digges, who, in reference to Shakespeare's tomb in the preface to the First Folio, writes, 'This book, when brass and marble fade, shall make thee look fresh to all ages.'

No, the museum curators might counter, as they point to artefacts such as the enigmatic 'Swimming Reindeer' carving, which dates back millennia before recorded script. The ancient civilisation that produced it may well have had the written word, but any such documentation is lost. No matter; 13,000 years later, this carving alone survives as proof of that culture's existence, and remains a work of art.

The conundrum of artistic beauty versus scientific truth also seems an eternal conflict. Can that question ever be resolved? The answer may lie both in the architecture of the British Museum, and in one of the greatest poetical works describing a typical artefact within. The pediment crowning the grand neo-classical entrance was carved by the nineteenth-century sculptor Richard Westmacott. Entitled The Progress of Civilisation, it depicts mankind's journey hand-in-hand with Art and Science. Perhaps this is also what Keats' was getting at in those final lines of 'Ode to a Grecian Urn':

> *Beauty is truth, truth beauty – that is all*
> *Ye know on earth, and all ye need to know.*

FURTHER READING

Exhibits right to left: Nereid monument; Easter Island statue; statue of A'a; Benin bronze; Lewis chessmen.

As *Romancing the British Museum* concentrates on the period at the height of the British empire, it only includes poems written up to the end of the nineteenth century, although more modern works have been referenced to make a point or reflect a theme. Of course, the exhibits in the British Museum continued to inspire poets throughout the twentieth and twenty-first centuries. Here are some of my favourites.

Note that some poems cannot be reproduced for reasons of copyright. However, I have listed published or online sources where they can be viewed.

The Great Court

Daljit Nagra, 'Meditations on the British Museum' (2017)

From Daljit Nagra, *British Museum*. Faber & Faber, 2017.
Daljit Nagra (born 1966) is a British poet with an Indian Sikh background. His book of poems *British Museum* was published in 2017.

The Reading Room

Richard Aldington, 'At the British Museum' (1929)

Find online here:

famouspoetsandpoems.com/poets/richard_aldington/poems/4352

John Masefield, 'The Reading Room' (1966)

Find online here:

theguardian.com/books/2005/jun/11/featuresreviews.guardianreview11

William Plomer, 'A Ticket for the Reading Room' (1940)

Find online here:

thepoeticalcorrectness.blogspot.com/2015/07/william-plomer-1903-1973-charles.html

Louis MacNeice, 'The British Museum Reading Room' (1939)

Find online here:

thelondoncolumn.com/2013/07/01/the-british-museum-reading-room

Parthenon Sculptures

Thomas Hardy, 'Christmas in the Elgin Room' (1928) (extracts)

> We are those whom Christmas overthrew
> Some centuries after Pheidias knew
> How to shape us, and bedrape us,
> And to set us in Athena's temple for men's view.
>
> Oh it is sad, now we are sold,
> We gods! For Borean people's gold,
> And brought to the gloom of this gaunt room,
> Which sunlight shuns and sweet Aurore but enters cold.

The last published poem of Thomas Hardy (1840–1928), 'Christmas in the Elgin Room', was also inspired by the ethical question of the Parthenon sculptures. This 1928 work sees a reversion to Byron's perspective.

Nereid Monument

H D, 'The Cliff Temple' (1916)

Find online here:

poets.org/poetsorg/poem/cliff-temple

According to the British Museum's publication *Forgotten Empire: The World of Ancient Persia*, the style of the Mausoleum at Halicarnassus was greatly inspired by the Nereid monument, which is situated nearby in Room 17.

The Nereid monument was so named because the female sculptures that stand between the columns reminded the nineteenth-century archaeologists of the Greek mythological sea-nymphs, the Nereids. The monument is thought to have been built as a tomb for Arbinas, Lycian ruler of Xanthos in the fifth century BC. It was excavated by British archaeologist Sir Charles Fellows and transported to the British Museum in 1848.

The monument, imagined in its native setting, was described in a poem entitled 'The Cliff Temple' (1916) by the American poet Hilda Doolittle (1886–1961), who worked under the signature 'H D'. In her novel *Asphodel*, she reveals that the monument in the museum was a favourite meeting place in her early romance with the Englishman and fellow poet Richard Aldington. Their poetry was associated with the imagist school. Championed by Ezra Pound (H D's former lover), the theory behind this modernist movement was that the poet worked in a direct free verse style to extract the essence of an image.

Indeed, the British Museum could be considered the birthplace of this genre. Not only was it influenced by the Greek and oriental exhibits, but it is said that during a meeting in 1912 with H D and Aldington in the museum tea room, Pound coined the term *Imagistes*. The inaugural anthology *Des Imagistes*, featuring works of H D and Aldington, was published by Pound in 1914.

Mummies

Frederic Rowland Marvin, 'Cleopatra's Mummy' (1907) (extracts)

A heap of crumbling bones,
Black with old Egypt's dust and grime;
A bit of shrivelled skin;
And painted cloth,
Brittle from years,
And with bitumen stained.

Once were these crumbling bones
Clothed in a woman's beauty,
More fragrant than the breath of incense
Burned where tinkling bells,
And crystal fountains,
Filled with gentle music
The whispering groves of fair Dodona,
And the pale-eyed priestess
Breathed the hallowed air.
Here rests the dark-eyed daughter of the Nile
Who nursed on golden bed
The sucking asp.

Thou wilt not come!
The lonely shadows deepen,
And from English sunset,
Dull and grey as sea-blown mists,
Dies the last flickering beam,
And all at length is still.
The visitors are gone:
The doors are closed:
The daughter of great Ptolemy,
In the London-town,
Slumbers unconscious of her shame.

Inspired by an Egyptian coffin with portrait, American poet and physician Frederic Rowland Marvin (1847–1918) devoted his lines to Cleopatra, a young woman from an influential Roman family. Her portrait is painted on the facial area of the linen bandage wrapped around her body. The inscription on her coffin tells us she died at the age of seventeen.

Easter Island Statue

Robert Frost, 'The Bad Island – Easter' (1962)

Find online here:

> *archive.org/stream/in.ernet.dli.2015.185708/2015.185708.In-The-Clearin
> g-By-Robert-Frost_djvu.txt*

The museum's Living and Dying Gallery exhibits sacred icons of belief, such as ancestry, gods and afterlife spirits. At the centre, proudly set on a plinth, is one of the famous Easter Island statues or *moai*. It is one of over 1,000 such statues that were dotted across the landscape of the South Pacific island locally known as Rapa Nui. The statues were carved from volcanic basalt rock. Some are over sixty feet tall and weigh up to four tons. Originally brightly painted, they are distinguished by their heavy brow, elongated ears, and sunken eyes where bright coral shells were once inserted. The back is covered in mysterious cult carvings. The meaning of the statues is not clear, but it is thought they offered some kind of ancestral protection.

Rapa Nui was discovered by Dutch explorers on Easter Day, 1722. With an area of just sixty-four square miles, it is the world's remotest place, 2,300 miles from Chile. Experts believe that in the twelfth century it thrived, with a population of up to 20,000, but by the nineteenth century it was almost deserted.

A definitive answer on why this happened has yet to be agreed. Many suggest some form of eco-disaster, brought about by a mixture of over-exploited resources, deforestation and the destruction of the steppe by the introduction of sheep. Others point to disease (perhaps smallpox introduced by Europeans) or a tsunami.

By 1888, when Chile took over administration, there were barely 150 people left. Their descendants make up the bulk of the modern islanders, and today Rapa Nui is one of the most studied islands in the world.

This particular statue, known as *Hoa Hakananai'a* ('secret friend'), is one of a pair that arrived in the museum in the late nineteenth century. In 1868, HMS *Topaze* visited the Juan Fernández islands to erect a memorial to Alexander Selkirk, the real-life Robinson Crusoe who was marooned there in the seventeenth century. Their next stop was Easter Island, 1,300 miles more remote! The captain negotiated with the locals to take two statues back to England. Two hundred islanders were required to load them onto the ship. During the voyage home, as they were strapped on board the open deck, the paint adorning the carvings weathered away. Both statues were presented to Queen Victoria, who subsequently gave them to the British Museum.

The statues have inspired a number of international poets, including the Australian Douglas Stewart (1913–85), the Canadian Frederick George Scott, known as the Poet of the Laurentians (1861–1944), and Nobel Prize-winning Chilean Pablo Neruda. All have written poems entitled 'Easter Island'. Pertaining to the actual statue in the museum, 'The Bad Island – Easter' (1962), by the pre-eminent American poet Robert Frost (1874–1963), certainly falls within the school that cries sorrow at the erasure of past cultures.

Statue of A'a (not always on display)

William Empson, 'Homage to the British Museum' (1932)

Find online here:

oatridge.co.uk/poems/w/william-empson-homage-to-the-british-museum. php

The wooden figure referred to by the British Museum as the statue of A'a is probably the most famous Polynesian sculpture in the world. Indeed, both Henry Moore and Pablo Picasso had casts made of the figure. Its fame, like other objects in the museum such as the Portland vase, stems largely from the argument as to its origin, meaning and purpose

It officially became part of the museum's collection in 1911 via the London Missionary Society, which in 1821 converted the inhabitants of the French Polynesian island of Rurutu to Christianity. Tribal chiefs are said to have handed over the carved deity as a symbol of their acceptance of their new faith. The 3ft 10in high figure is a composite of a male form and thirty smaller carved human figures that form bodily features. The main body was hollowed out and once contained twenty-four figurines accessed by a carved removable panel at the back. These are now lost, but they may not originally have been meant to be placed here, as the cavity may have been used as a reliquary for real human bones. Curators did find a small red bird feather and a strand of human hair inside the hollow interior, and such remains of fibrous materials are consistent with Polynesian sacred beliefs.

The ambiguity of its origins is down to a variety of reasons. As the figure seemingly depicts a process of creating other beings, it has been identified as the divine creator known in Polynesian lore as A'a, Tangaroa or Taaroa. Radiocarbon tests date the wood to the sixteenth century, but the statue's long history means its religious purpose may well have been subject to continuous change. Also, some native customs were almost certainly lost during a sustained period of social turmoil immediately before the islanders' conversion to Christianity. Some regard 'A'a' is the sole surviving indigenous deity, as all the other ancient religious symbols were ritually cremated on conversion. However, several other figures collected by missionaries survive. Tribal chiefs also dispute the tested fact that it is carved from sandalwood, preferring their own tradition that the statue was carved from the pua or 'perfume flower tree'. The oral tradition of the Rurutu culture means that a lack of written records contributes to the debate.

The esteemed literary critic William Empson (1906–84) published his poem 'Homage to the British Museum' in 1932. His opening line, 'There is a supreme God in the ethnological section,' suggests his dismay, in much the same vein as Rossetti's 'Burden of Nineveh', that as soon as such a symbolic icon – indeed, a 'supreme god' – is captured as an exhibit, it represents the negation and subjugation of a whole ethnic culture.

However, and typically ambivalent of Empson, while accepting the statue as a local almighty on the one hand, he also goes with a theory that the figure may be an amalgamation of other deities. And, even if this great being has been homogenised, Man might allow him to rule locally again. As such, it could be argued that Empson is justifying the ways of Man to God.

The poem was displayed on the London Underground in commemoration of the British Museum's 250th anniversary in 2009.

Benin Bronzes (not always on display)

George the Poet, 'The Benin Bronze' (2015)

A spoken version narrated by George himself can be found online here:

youtube.com/watch?v=3IlUMUGUorw

The Benin bronzes are a collection of reliefs and sculptures that originally decorated the royal palace of the kingdom of Benin in what is now Nigeria. The kingdom operated from the twelfth to the end of the nineteenth century when it was annexed by the British empire. In 1897, the Benin royal palace was looted by a British expeditionary force. Two hundred decorative bronze reliefs were taken and eventually found their way to the British Museum. The plaques illustrate the history of the Benin kingdom in the fifteenth and sixteenth centuries. The majority depict royal dignitaries wearing ceremonial dress, warriors, and animals such as the leopard. Collectively, they form the best-known example of Benin art. In an international dispute over restitution, comparable to that of the Elgin Marbles, Nigeria has sought the return of these artefacts.

The British George Mpanga (born 1991), also known as George the Poet, was invited by the British Museum in 2015 to write a poem on the Benin bronzes. He pulled no punches in telling the violent story of how the museum acquired them.

Lewis Chessmen

Gillian Spraggs, 'The Lewis Chessmen' (1994)

Find online here:

gillianspraggs.com/poems/lewis.html

The Lewis chessmen are the oldest proper chess set ever found. They were found by accident in 1831 in Uig, Isle of Lewis, Scotland, in a small drystone chamber under a sand dune. Carved from walrus tusk and whale teeth, they are dated to some point after 1150, simply by surmising that the church decreed in that year that the bishop's mitre should point forwards.

Some experts suggest they may have been in the possession of a salesman travelling from Norway to Ireland. There is much evidence for this theory: Lewis was part of the kingdom of Norway until 1266, and a Norwegian ivory reliquary in the British Museum is modelled and carved the same way. Also, a similar chess piece was found in an Irish bog. In addition, there were enough kings for four sets, and the find included other carved pieces for draughts and belt buckles. Finally, all the sets are in excellent condition, probably unused.

A set would have been very expensive. It is estimated it would have taken six tusks to make one full game. They were tough to carve. Each piece is sculpted differently, and they are elaborately worked. For example, the queen sits on a throne, making very visible and powerful gestures of either despair or boredom. She also holds a drinking horn. The knights are mounted. The 'rooks' are warriors known as berserkers. They are biting their shields in order to build themselves up into a frenzy before a battle. The pawns are inanimate tombstones, perhaps representing the expendability of foot soldiers. Some pieces were stained red, indicating the chessboard may have been red and white.

It is believed the game of chess was invented in India around the year 600 and moved westwards over centuries. When chess pieces reached Europe in the twelfth century as geometric shapes, modern rules were written and a template for the pieces was designed. It reflected feudal society at the crossroads of paganism and Christianity. The game became part of the medieval chivalric code alongside hawking and verse writing.

The Lewis chessmen served as models for the wizard chess set in the *Harry Potter* movies. They also inspired the children's television series *Noggin the Nog* by Peter Firmin.

'The Lewis Chessmen', a poem by Gillian Spraggs (born 1952), was published in *As Girls Could Boast: New Poetry by Women* (ed. Christina Dunhill, Oscars Press, 1994). It describes the character of each carved piece and the shock of seeing them for the first time in the museum, with them glaring back at her.

GHOSTS OF SWINGING LONDON

From Tin Pan Alley to Carnaby Street

INTRODUCTION

This jaunt through London's Soho pays its respects to lost music venues of the sixties, visiting pubs once frequented by rock 'n' roll legends, backed by a swinging soundtrack along the way. The itinerary is based on *London's Original Rock 'n' Roll Pub Walk*, which the author officially devised for the National Portrait Gallery's 2009 exhibition *From the Beatles to Bowie.*

Swinging London

When rock 'n' roll first hit the airwaves in the mid-fifties, London was a grim, austere city, still reeling from World War II destruction and the resultant food rationing. Living standards were down 50% against pre-war records and around 60% of the population lived below the poverty line. For young people, there were limited breaks from the stifling drudgery. At the weekend, perhaps going to a football match or a dance, or having a singalong in the pub. And, in the summertime, maybe a week in a holiday camp.

Over the next decade a revolution took place, and by 1966 London had been labelled the world's capital of culture. Social historians point to a number of reasons for this remarkable transformation, including a vibrant youth scene (in 1960, 50% of Londoners were under thirty), relaxed attitudes (the so-called permissive society), and disposable incomes tied in with a consumer credit boom. The soundtrack to this fast-shifting age came in cheap and convenient forms, in the medium of both the portable transistor radio and the vinyl seven-inch single. Suddenly, popular music could provide instant escapism: a fanfare for the common man and woman.

The heartbeat of the swinging sixties in the capital was Soho. The previous decade had seen the American-influenced jazz, blues and folk clubs here form the roots of a very British rock 'n' roll revolution. Now it had become London's Bohemian rhapsody, with artists, musicians and media types contributing to a lively bar and café culture, combined with a red-light district and an emerging gay scene. The area was packed with dens of entertainment, naughtiness and musical talent. The lyrics from pop songs such as David Bowie's 'London Boys', the Who's 'Pinball

Wizard' and the Kinks' 'Lola' bear this reputation out.

Now, almost all the old haunts are gone. The last recording studio on Tin Pan Alley has shut down; authorities rarely grant music licences; the area has been redeveloped, gentrified and homogenised. All we have left are the ghosts ...

Soundtrack

All songs date from 1960 to 1970 and can be found on most music apps.

1. The Kinks, 'Denmark Street' (1970)
2. Simon & Garfunkel, 'Homeward Bound' (1965)
3. Fairport Convention, 'Who Knows Where the Time Goes?' (1969)
4. Bob Dylan, 'Like a Rolling Stone' (1965)
5. Rolling Stones, 'I Wanna Be Your Man' (1963)
6. Small Faces, 'Sha-La-La-La-Lee' (1966)
7. Georgie Fame and the Blue Flames, 'Yeh Yeh' (1964)
8. Desmond Dekker, 'The Israelites' (1968)
9. Led Zeppelin, 'Whole Lotta Love' (1969)
10. Pink Floyd, 'See Emily Play' (1967)
11. The Shadows, 'Apache' (1960)
12. Cream, 'I Feel Free' (1966)
13. Fleetwood Mac, 'Albatross' (1968)
14. David Bowie, 'London Boys' (1966)
15. The Who, 'Pinball Wizard' (1969)
16. The Beatles, 'Hey Jude' (1967)
17. The Jimi Hendrix Experience, 'Foxy Lady' (1967)
18. Johnny Kidd & the Pirates, 'Shakin' All Over' (1960)
19. Small Faces, 'All or Nothing' (1966)
20. The Kinks, 'Dedicated Follower of Fashion' (1966)

POINT 1: DENMARK STREET: TIN PAN ALLEY

Route: Start at Tottenham Court Road tube station. Walk down Charing Cross Road and turn left onto Denmark Street.

Song: Kinks, 'Denmark Street'

Denmark Street

Denmark Street, also known as 'Tin Pan Alley', was swinging London's pop music HQ. Anyone who was anyone on the sixties scene could have been spotted at the various recording studios or instrument stores at one time or another. With music publishers and impresarios also based here, it was the scene of many an acrimonious argument between band and management: a theme reflected in the Kinks song 'Denmark Street', written at the end of the decade.

4 Denmark Street (Regent Studios)

Regent Studios was established in 1963 as a tiny recording studio with primitive egg-carton soundproofing. The Rolling Stones were the first major band to record an album here in 1964, followed by the quintessential swinging London band, the Kinks, who recorded their first tracks here as the Ravens. It was also where the young Elton John recorded covers for Woolworth's Embassy Records. In 1970, Black Sabbath recorded *Paranoid* here, heralding the heavy metal genre.

5 Denmark Street (New Musical Express offices)

New Musical Express was responsible for publishing the first official UK charts in 1952.

9 Denmark Street (Giaconda)

The Small Faces often came to the Giaconda café. In 1965 David Bowie lived in a van outside, forming his first band in the café.

11 Denmark Street (Rose Morris Music)

Rose Morris Music was established in the 1920s as the first music shop on Denmark Street. The Moody Blues were regular shoppers here.

19 Denmark Street (Melody Maker offices)

The music paper *Melody Maker*, established in 1926, helped form many a band through its popular ads section.

20 Denmark Street (Mills Music)

The young Elton John was an office gofer for Mills Music publishers. The company rejected Paul Simon's 'Sound of Silence' and 'Homeward Bound', so Simon started his own publisher, Charing Cross Music (named after the main road nearby), and has owned the rights to his music ever since.

22 Denmark Street (Rhodes Music)

Sold guitars to Jeff Beck, Eric Clapton and Pete Townsend. In the basement was Tin Pan Alley Studios, which heard recordings by Manfred Mann, Jimi Hendrix and Simon & Garfunkel, among others.

25 Denmark Street (Denmark Productions)

The Kinks and Troggs recorded here.

27 Denmark Street (Andy's Guitar Shop)

Andy's Guitar Shop saw custom from Jimmy Page and the Kinks.

132 Charing Cross Road (Northern Songs)

The publisher Northern Songs owned the Beatles' song rights.

POINT 2: MOOR STREET: THE SPICE OF LIFE

Route: From Denmark Street, turn left onto Charing Cross Road. Walk a short distance and turn right onto Moor Street.

Songs: Simon & Garfunkel, 'Homeward Bound'; Fairport Convention, 'Who Knows Where the Time Goes?'

6 Moor Street (Spice of Life/Scots Hoose)

There has been a pub on this site since 1750. In 1952, when it was known as the Scots Hoose, the first folk club in London was established upstairs and forged a good reputation.

Folk legends who played here include Cat Stevens, Leonard Cohen and Bob Dylan. On 22 January 1965, Paul Simon performed here. He was about to embark on a gruelling nationwide tour of British folk clubs, the end of which would result in the penning of his first UK hit, 'Homeward Bound'.

Another folk hero who often performed here was the south London songstress Sandy Denny, who would go on to become the lead singer of Fairport Convention. Denny, who died in 1978 at the age of just thirty-one, is still regarded as the UK's first prominent female singer-songwriter.

Live gigs still take place today in the basement.

POINT 3: GREAT NEWPORT STREET: THE PORCUPINE

Route: From Moor Street, turn right onto Charing Cross Road and left onto Litchfield Street. Then return to Charing Cross Road and turn left. After a short distance, turn left onto Great Newport Street.

Songs: Bob Dylan, 'Like a Rolling Stone'; Rolling Stones, 'I Wanna Be Your Man'

27 Litchfield Street (Bunjies Folk Club)

Opened in the early fifties, the basement venue featured the likes of Paul Simon, Cat Stevens and Al Stewart watched by audiences that included Phil Collins, David Bowie and Rod Stewart. In 1962, Bob Dylan played this tiny club during his first tour of the UK as a relatively unknown songster. Three years later, during his sell-out second tour of the country, Dylan wrote 'Like a Rolling Stone', based on his original travails as a 'complete unknown'. It was his biggest UK hit.

11 Great Newport Street (Studio 51)

A plaque marks the site of a jazz club that opened in the basement in 1951. A skiffle section, with music played on homemade instruments, such as a washboard, spoons and a tea chest, was introduced. Skiffle had a major impact on British rock 'n' roll and formed the roots of many bands such as the Beatles, the Who and the Rolling Stones. Indeed, the Rolling Stones became the resident band at this spot, playing over forty gigs here in 1963: more than they have played at any other venue. The Yardbirds were also regular performers.

12 Great Newport Street (Bruce Fleming photographic studio)

The cover for the 1967 Jimi Hendrix album *Are You Experienced* was shot on the third floor.

15 Great Newport Street (Pickwick Club)

Opened in 1963 and owned by the entertainer Harry Secombe. Visitors included Frank Sinatra and the Beatles. Johnny Cash played here in 1966.

48 Charing Cross Road (The Porcupine)

Studio 51 had no licence to sell alcohol, so musicians often popped into this pub before and after gigs. It forged a reputation for attracting harmonica players, including Rod Stewart and Bob Dylan. Among those who played here was Charlie Perez, a blues harp player who played with all the greats. His love for the instrument made him change his name to Charlie Harper. He went on to form the punk band UK Subs in 1976.

Paul McCartney relates a fascinating episode that occurred on this street in September 1963. He shared a taxi here with John Lennon, Mick Jagger and Keith Richards. Jagger told them they were recording a demo and asked for any songs. John and Paul offered them the unfinished 'I Wanna Be Your Man'. While they were watching, the Stones tried it out at Studio 51. However, they complained there was no middle section. John and Paul went to the Porcupine pub, wrote one out in five minutes and came back to perform it. It wasn't difficult; it was a simple song. Nonetheless, the Stones were dumbstruck. The Stones cut a sharp studio rendition of the song, which became their first top 20 hit.

POINT 4: WARDOUR STREET: O'NEILL'S

Route: From Great Newport Street, cross Charing Cross Rd onto Little Newport Street/Lisle Street. Turn left onto Leicester Place. Then return to Lisle Street, go left, turn right onto Wardour Street and walk to junction with Gerrard Street.

Songs: Small Faces, 'Sha-La-La-La-Lee'; Georgie Fame, 'Yeh Yeh'; Desmond Dekker, 'The Israelites'

6 Leicester Place (The Cavern)

Known as the Cavern in the Town, and based on the Cavern Club in Liverpool. London-based group the Small Faces became resident band here in 1965.

33 Wardour Street (The Flamingo)

In London's Chinatown is a basement entrance next to a typical Irish 'theme' pub. Nothing remarkable to the passing visitor, apart from a plaque reminding us that this was once one of the world's greatest music venues.

Feel the ghosts! Starting as an all-nighter bar underneath the Whisky-a-Go-Go club in the 1960s, surely no other venue was at the forefront of so many different soundwaves of popular music. The line of performers under its various incarnations as the Flamingo, the Temple and the Wag Club reads like a hall of fame. From the world of blues, John Lee Hooker, Bo Diddley and BB King. Soulsters, Stevie Wonder, Otis Redding and Wilson Pickett. Sixties rock legends, the Who, Animals, Yardbirds, Small Faces, Moody Blues and Jimi Hendrix. Seventies rock legends, Deep Purple, Black Sabbath, Led Zeppelin, Thin Lizzy, Supertramp and Genesis. In the 1980s, David Bowie filmed his 'Blue Jean' video here, ushering in the New Romantic era. Hip-hop was represented by Afrika Bambaataa, Grandmaster Flash and Doug E Fresh, and house by Marshall Jefferson, Frankie Knuckles and Todd Terry. With that weight of legacy, it's no surprise that the place was labelled 'the grooviest club on the planet'.

But let's go way back to the early sixties. Back before 1964, when Simon & Garfunkel made their UK debut here, and back before 1963, when the classic line-up of the Rolling Stones chose this venue for their full first outing on stage. In 1962, R&B outfit Georgie Fame and the Blue Flames had just begun a three-year stint as the 'Mingo's' resident band. Often performing with them on stage was a Jamaican jazz musician known as 'Syco' Gordon, whose brother 'Lucky' was also a regular at the club. One October night, a nasty brawl on the dancefloor saw Lucky end up with seventeen stitches. He had been attacked in an argument over a high-society call girl. The girl in question was Christine Keeler. The incident led to a chain of events that culminated in the infamous political scandal known as the Profumo affair.

Lucky went on to work for Chris Blackwell at the record company Island. In 1963, the label had its first UK hit, Millie Small's ska version of 'My Boy Lollipop'. Millie dated Peter Asher of the pop duo Peter and Gordon. For a while, she stayed at his parents' home at 57 Wimpole Street, Marylebone, with Peter's sister Jane, and Jane's boyfriend, Paul McCartney, who was in the process of composing *Yesterday*.

Four years later, just before his break-up with Jane, McCartney penned the Beatles' ska-flavoured 'Ob La Di, Ob La Da'. The title is an ode to a favourite saying of McCartney's associate, the African conga musician Jimmy Scott, who often performed at the Flamingo. The song mentions a Desmond, referring to ska legend Desmond Dekker of 'Israelites' fame. Dekker was performing in the Flamingo on the evening of the infamous fight.

POINT 5: MACCLESFIELD STREET (CHINATOWN): DE HEMS

Route: From Wardour Street, turn right onto Gerrard Street. Halfway down Gerrard Street, turn onto Macclesfield Street.

Songs: Led Zeppelin, 'Whole Lotta Love'; Pink Floyd, 'See Emily Play'.

Chinatown

London's Chinese community, originally based in the Limehouse area of the East End, moved to this part of the city in the mid-twentieth century. On New Year's Eve 1963, the Kinks got their first big break playing a gig at the China Garden restaurant, impressing agent Arthur Howe. In one of the basements of Chinatown (no one is sure which), the New Yardbirds, featuring Jimmy Page, Robert Plant, John Bonham and John Paul Jones, held their first rehearsal in August 1968. Within weeks they would change their name to Led Zeppelin. Jones recalled, 'We first played together in a small basement room in Gerrard Street. There was just wall-to-wall amplifiers, Marshalls everywhere, and a space for the door, and that was it.'

39 Gerrard Street (Ronnie Scott's, 1959–65)

Jazz club where John Lennon celebrated his twenty-third birthday in 1963. In 1965, Scott's reopened on Frith Street in Soho, and it has remained the epicentre of the London jazz scene ever since. Scott played saxophone on the Beatles' 'Lady Madonna' in 1968.

43–44 Gerrard Street (Happening 44)

Established in the 1920s as the notorious 43 Club, by the early fifties it had become George Melly's West End Jazz Club. The word *rave* is said to have been coined here. In the late sixties, it was transformed into one of the first psychedelic clubs, Happening 44. Fairport Convention played early gigs here, as did Pink Floyd, led by Syd Barrett. Barrett lived around the corner on Earlham Street, where he wrote most of his songs in a hallucinogenic haze.

11 Macclesfield Street (De Hems)

Music business watering hole. The *Record Mirror* publishing offices were just around the corner on Shaftesbury Avenue. Artists were often bought here after interviews, including the Kinks, the Hollies and Herman's Hermits. Other regular patrons were Georgie Fame, Alan Price of the Animals, and Phil Spector.

Many band management deals took place on the premises, including negotiations for the Rolling Stones and the Who. The Beach Boys drummer Dennis Wilson tried to get a record contract here for an American songwriter lodging at his home in California: one Charles Manson.

POINT 6: OLD COMPTON STREET: COMPTON'S

Route: From Macclesfield Street turn right onto Shaftesbury Avenue. Turn left onto Frith Street, then left onto Old Compton Street.

Song: Shadows, 'Apache'

Frith Street

Frith Street became synonymous with coffee bar culture back in the 1950s. Indeed, it was known as Froth Street in its heyday. It was a scene particularly attractive to youngsters, as they could gather in relatively inexpensive social venues without alcohol and sing and dance to music. Moka, opened in 1953 by Italian actress Gina Lollobrigida at No. 29, was the first to have a proper espresso machine. Bar Italia, at No. 22, is still operating today on the same site.

51–53 Old Compton Street (Swiss Tavern)

For most of its 130-year history, 'The Grand Dame of Soho', as it has been dubbed, has been regarded as a gay drinking establishment. Known as the Swiss in its heyday, it is currently named Comptons, and still attracts a varied gay crowd, alongside many tourists. It was here in 1958 that Harry Webb and his backing band made the decision to become Cliff Richard and the Drifters (later the Shadows).

59 Old Compton Street (2 i's)

Birthplace of British rock 'n' roll, also known as 'the home of the stars'. The basement of this property was turned into a nightclub in 1956. The songwriter Lionel Bart designed the stage, and his connections attracted all the most important impresarios. It soon became the most famous music venue in the UK, inspiring, it is claimed, the legendary Cavern Club in Liverpool.

Tommy Steele, Britain's first genuine pop idol, sang here on the opening night. The next day he sealed a record contract.

The first UK TV pop show, *Six-Five Special*, was filmed here in 1957. The same year, Cliff Richard performed here. His impact on British rock 'n' roll is rarely highlighted. He claims the very first live recorded rock 'n' roll album, *Cliff*, and the first UK-written rock 'n' roll hit, 'Move It'. By the time the Beatles hit big, Cliff had amassed twenty-three UK hits, including seven number ones. He would go on to become the UK's most successful pop artist. Cliff's backing band emerged in their own right to become the UK's biggest-selling instrumental group, the Shadows, with thirty-one UK hits in the sixties, including five number ones.

A much less mainstream rock 'n' roll performer was Vince Taylor, who formed his band the Playboys here. Barely known in the UK, he became a godlike cult idol in France. Taylor was managed by his brother-in-law Joe Barbera of Hannah-Barbera cartoon fame, and his antics became legendary. For example, unlike the Who, who gained a reputation by wrecking the stage after a set, Taylor would destroy it *beforehand*. He was a major inspiration behind Bowie's creation Ziggy Stardust.

63 Old Compton Street (Millings & Son)

In early 1963, Beatles manager Brian Epstein asked this tailor to come up with a distinctive suit design. The result was the collarless 'Beatle suits' in four colours, and 500 more outfits for the band.

76 Old Compton Street (Norman's Film Productions)

Bang opposite is a place where the Beatles spent much time in the late sixties. Here on the second floor, they came practically every weekday for eleven weeks in late 1967 to edit their *Magical Mystery Tour* movie. Aside from Abbey Road, they probably visited Old Compton Street more than any other street in London.

POINT 7: WARDOUR STREET: RESIDENCE BAR

Route: Turn right onto Wardour Street and walk to junction with Brewer Street.

Songs: Cream, 'I Feel Free'; Fleetwood Mac, 'Albatross'

83 Wardour St (Roundhouse)

In 1954, blues musician Cyril Davies opened the London Skiffle Club above this pub. When the skiffle craze faded, Davies asked fellow musician Alexis Korner to open the Blues & Barrelhouse Club in the same venue. Barrelhouse was a form of boogie-woogie.

This place then became the most influential venue in the development of British rock. All the great blues artists came here, including the legendary Muddy Waters, who in 1958 shocked the audience by *plugging in* his guitar, and by doing so starting a revolution.

Korner subsequently started a band called Blues Incorporated which included, at various times, Charlie Watts, Mick Jagger, Keith Richards, Brian Jones, Jimmy Page, Jack Bruce and Ginger Baker. As such, this pub was the breeding ground for the Rolling Stones, Led Zeppelin and the 'supergroup' Cream. Another significant member was John Mayall, who formed his own band, the Bluesbreakers. A 1967 reshuffle of this group saw three other musicians join: Peter Green, Mick Fleetwood and John McVie, who then formed Fleetwood Mac, the most commercially successful British blues group. Within a year they had recorded their number one single 'Albatross'.

POINT 8: WARDOUR STREET: THE SHIP

Route: Continue northwards on Wardour Street to junction with Flaxman Court.

Songs: David Bowie, 'London Boys'; Who, Pinball Wizard'

90 Wardour Street (Marquee)

Possibly the most important venue in the history of British rock. The original Marquee jazz and blues club opened on Oxford Street in 1958. Members included Eric Clapton, Jimmy Page and Keith Richards. On 12 July 1962 Richards and friends played their first formal gig as the Rollin' Stones.

The club relocated to Wardour Street in 1964. Its awning featuring the famous red and white striped circus design was created by photographer Angus McBean. It saw London debuts for David Bowie and Led Zeppelin. Resident bands through the sixties read like a *Who's Who* of rock: Manfred Mann, Yardbirds, Spencer Davies Group, Rod Stewart and the Soul Agents, Small Faces, Cream, Pink Floyd and Procol Harum. But the band most synonymous with the Marquee during the sixties was the Who. Formed in Acton, west London, in 1964, the classic line-up of Roger

Daltrey, Pete Townshend, John Entwistle and Keith Moon went on to score fourteen UK hits in the 1960s.

In 1988, it was decided that the vibrations of the music had made the building unsafe (how rock 'n' roll is that?) and it was demolished. Since that time, it has reopened in various locations. It was last seen in Covent Garden in 2008.

100 Wardour Street (La Chasse)

After a gig at the Marquee it was difficult to get a drink as the pubs were shut. But, for those artists in the know, there were a number of illicit after-hours drinking clubs in the area. La Chasse, for example, was a tiny smoky first-floor room above No. 100 Wardour Street, with a bar, a jukebox and room for about thirty people. Here, manager Jack Barry would ladle out his homemade goulash to hungry post-gig luminaries such as Elton John, David Bowie and Rod Stewart.

116 Wardour Street (The Ship)

Famous London rock 'n' roll pub. As the Marquee was not licensed, many rock artists drank here before gigs. Major music deals were done in this pub. Sixties patrons include John Lennon, Syd Barrett, Jimi Hendrix (who passed out in the corner) and Keith Moon (who was barred after letting off a smoke bomb).

POINT 9: D'ARBLAY STREET: THE GEORGE

Route: Follow Flaxman Court around the corner to St Anne's Court. Then turn right onto Wardour Street and walk to the junction with D'Arblay Street.

Songs: Beatles, 'Hey Jude'; Jimi Hendrix Experience, 'Foxy Lady'

20 St Anne's Court

Some Beatles biographies attest that the Blue Gardenia club was based here, although others claim it was sited in Wardour Mews off D'Arblay Street.

The Blue Gardenia was a basement club where bands came to relax after gigs in the early sixties. It was run by Brian Casser, a Liverpool-based singer who had formed a skiffle group with Bill Wyman in the late fifties.

On 9 December 1961, Casser welcomed a young up-and-coming band from Liverpool to his London club. He knew the band well. A year earlier, his own band the Cassanovas had shared a stage with them on the same bill, only then they were known as the Silver Beetles. On this particular winter's night, the Beatles were returning from their first south-of-England public performance in the army town of Aldershot. It had been a disaster: just eighteen people turned up, the band got drunk on stage, the police were called and the band ordered to leave. It has been referred to in Beatles lore as the 'lost gig'. To cheer themselves up they headed to London's Blue Gardenia club. Casser claimed Georgie Fame was in the club that night and encouraged these late guests to jam with him. Lennon and McCartney got up on the tiny stage with Pete Best on drums (but minus Harrison, who sat drinking) to deliver an impromptu performance. The Beatles had made their first ever London appearance. The band left at 5 am and drove all the way back to Liverpool.

17 St Anne's Court (Trident Studios)

In 1967, a few yards along the same passageway, a pioneering recording facility with a revolutionary eight-track mixing desk was opened, Trident Studios. It was here that the Beatles recorded many tracks of their seminal 'White Album', having dispensed with the services of Abbey Road. Seven years had passed since that narrow little alleyway resounded to the muted after-hours appearance of a little-known band from north-west England. Now they had returned, and the alleyway echoed to their sound once again. But this time, they were the biggest band in the world.

Other legendary rock albums recorded here include David Bowie's *Ziggy Stardust* and Lou Reed's *Transformer*. An ancient Bechstein piano that once sat in the studio was the same instrument heard on Elton John's 'Rocket Man' and Queen's 'Bohemian Rhapsody'. It was also the same one used on the opening bars of the Beatles' epic 1968 single 'Hey Jude'.

1 D'Arblay Street (The George)

One of the oldest pubs in Soho, dating back almost 300 years. In the early fifties, Welsh poet Dylan Thomas is said to have collapsed here after a fight with a jazz musician and was eventually ejected for being drunk and disorderly.

During the sixties the pub had a mellower reputation than its noisy neighbour, the Ship. Nevertheless, the George has a small share of rock history. It was a haunt of the Jimi Hendrix Experience, Noel Redding being a regular. It was also one of the favourite drinking holes of record company boss Tony Stratton-Smith, who founded the Charisma label in 1969. After promptly signing up Genesis he began negotiations with Lindisfarne in this pub.

POINT 10: GREAT MARLBOROUGH STREET: COACH & HORSES

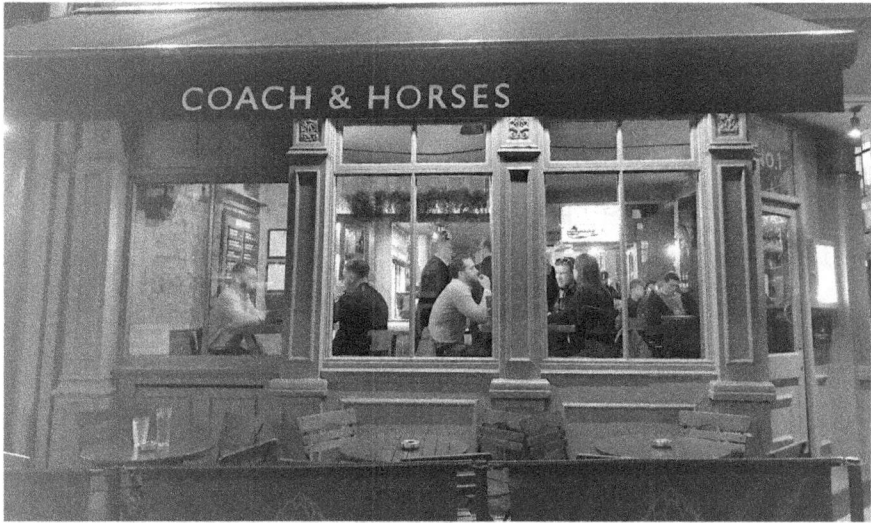

Route: Continue northwards on Wardour Street. Turn left onto Noel Street and walk to junction with Berwick Street. Continue westwards on Noel Street to Great Marlborough Street.

Songs: Johnny Kidd & The Pirates, 'Shakin' All Over'

44 Berwick Street (Freight Train)

In the late 1950s, this was the location of Freight Train, a coffee bar opened by Chas McDevitt on the proceeds of his skiffle hit of the same name. The early TV pop show *Six-Five Special* was once broadcast from here.

Many of the acts who performed in this venue were from the stable of the impresario Larry Parnes. They made their names recording British covers of American hits before the US companies had the chance to release originals in the UK. Parnes chose descriptive names for his acts such as Billy Fury (Ron Wycherley), Adam Faith (Terry Nelhams) and Marty Wilde (Reg Smith). Joe Brown wisely rejected Parnes's stage name of Elmer Twitch.

In the 1960s the site became a record shop employing Elton John (when he was plain Reg Dwight). The record stores of Berwick Street helped the area remain a focal hub of the music industry right up until the new millennium. Indeed, if you look south from this standpoint you may recognise the view as the cover design for one of the bestselling rock albums of all time, Oasis's 1995 *What's the Story, Morning Glory*?

Fred Heath, lead singer of Johnny Kidd & the Pirates, wrote the song 'Shakin' All Over' here. In 1960, it became the first UK-penned rock 'n' roll single to become a hit in the USA. The band had nine UK hits between 1959 and 1964 before Heath was killed in a car crash in 1966, returning from a cancelled gig.

The drummer on the single is the most unsung hero of British rock 'n' roll. Born in north London in 1937, Clem Cattini has featured on more number one singles than anyone else. Apart from 'Shakin' All Over', Cattini's sixties number ones include 'It's Not Unusual', 'The Sun Ain't Gonna Shine (Anymore)', 'You Don't Have to Say You Love Me', 'Please Release Me' and 'Where Do You Go To (My Lovely)?'. He also drummed on 'Telstar', the instrumental hit by the Tornados which was the first UK-written rock 'n' roll song to reach number one in the USA.

1 Great Marlborough Street (Coach & Horses)

Around the corner from this pub, at 155 Oxford Street, were the offices of record labels Chrysalis and Island. Their stable of bands in the late sixties included Free, Jethro Tull, Mott the Hoople and Procol Harum.

The Coach & Horses was also the favourite haunt of hellraising Led Zeppelin drummer John Bonham, who would plan his days of mayhem here. He would gang up with other musicians, then get the barmaid to mix some lethal cocktails of liquors and brandies and give them to the record company management. Bonham died in 1980, aged thirty-two.

POINT 11: CARNABY STREET: SHAKESPEARE'S HEAD

Route: Continue westwards on Great Marlborough Street, then turn left onto Carnaby Street. Foubert's Place is off Carnaby Street.

Songs: Small Faces, 'All or Nothing'; Kinks, 'Dedicated Follower of Fashion'.

Carnaby Street

Carnaby Street derives its name from the locally sited Karnaby House, which dated back to the 1680s. In the 1960s, along with the King's Road in Chelsea, it was *the* place to go shopping for London's dedicated followers of fashion (or 'Carnabetians', as labelled in the Kinks song). Many independent boutiques that began on this street went on to become major brands, including Lord John, Cecil Gee and Ravel. The April 1966 issue of *Time* magazine noted how this street had become the epicentre of a cultural revolution:

> *Perhaps nothing illustrates the new swinging London better than Carnaby Street, which is crammed with a cluster of boutiques. But London is not keeping the good news to itself. From Carnaby Street, the new, way-out fashion is spreading around the globe.*

1 Carnaby Street

Plaque to fashion entrepreneur John Stephen, 'the king of Carnaby Street' and driving force in the evolution of sixties pop culture.

5 Carnaby Street (His)

John Stephen opened a menswear shop called His in 1958. It became a mecca for London's emerging 'mod' culture. By 1966 he owned nine other shops on the street, including Mod Male and Male West One. Stephen also dressed women, with Petula Clark, Elizabeth Taylor and Marlene Dietrich among his clients.

52–55 Carnaby Street

Plaque dedicated to Don Arden and the Small Faces.

The Small Faces were a London-based band featuring Steve Marriott, Ronnie Lane, Kenney Jones and Jimmy Winston (replaced by Ian McLagan). From 1965 to 1969 they had twelve hits, including the number one 'All or Nothing'.

Arden (1926–2007) was a music impresario whose aggressive tactics led to his being nicknamed the 'Al Capone of Pop'. He signed the band here in 1965, then allegedly spent £12,000 fixing their first chart hit. Two years later he sold them to the Rolling Stones' manager Andrew Loog Oldham for £25,000 cash, delivered in a brown paper bag.

Later, Arden started his own record label, Jet Records, signing Black Sabbath. The lead singer, Ozzy Osbourne, married Arden's daughter Sharon, alienating her from her father.

15 Foubert's Place (I Was Lord Kitchener's Valet)

This boutique sold antique military uniforms as fashion items. The original store was opened on Portobello Road in Notting Hill in 1965, and it later had another branch on the King's Road in Chelsea. Sixties pop celebrities who frequented the shops were Jimi Hendrix, the Who and the Beatles. Peter Blake, who designed the *Sgt Pepper* album cover, said that he got the uniform idea while walking past the shop.

Shakespeare's Head, Carnaby Street

Of the many Carnaby Street luminaries who must surely have had a drink in this establishment in its sixties heyday, Billy J Kramer, the Fourmost, Dave Davies of the Kinks, Rod Stewart and John Lennon are actually on the record.

POINT 12: FINISH AND POSTSCRIPT

Let us end with a tale relating to the two great sentinels of the swinging sixties: the Beatles and the Stones.

Finishing this walk at Oxford Circus tube station via Argyll Street, you will pass by the London Palladium. This famous venue opened as a music hall in 1910, becoming a theatre in the 1920s. All the jazz greats have appeared here, including Duke Ellington and Ella Fitzgerald. In the 1960s, it played host to *Sunday Night at the London Palladium*, a TV programme showcasing the best of British showbiz talent. On Sunday 13 October 1963, the Beatles topped the bill. Fifteen million people watched the show on TV. They became an overnight sensation and Beatlemania was born.

Unlike the Beatles, the Rolling Stones initially refused to appear on the *London Palladium* TV show, which they considered too square for their rebel image. Under pressure from management, they finally relented in 1967. But when it came to joining their fellow performers on the stage at the end of the show, the Stones refused. The decision caused outrage in the press, boosting their bad-boy image.

Even though we've only covered the relatively small area of Soho on this walk, that little vignette tells us something: that in the decade that defined the popular music genre more than any other, the battleground for all these singers, musicians and bands – arguing over contracts, fighting for airtime, vying for stage appearances, competing for press coverage and, ultimately, trying to make it big – was London.

So, which is the greatest rock 'n' roll city? If you've always presumed that the answer lies somewhere between the east and west coasts of America, I hope that, by taking you by the hand and leading you through the streets of London, I've shown you something to make you change your mind.

SOURCES & REFERENCES

SOUL CITY WANDERING

Introduction

Image

Boudicca, Westminster Bridge. Copyright: the author.

Poems

Betjeman, John. 'Metro-Land'. Murray, 1973.
Betjeman, John. 'The Cockney Amorist'. *Collected Poems.* Murray, 2006.
Eliot, T S. *The Waste Land.* Faber & Faber, 2002.
Frost, Robert. 'The Road Not Taken'. *A Collection.* CreateSpace, 2010.
Gay, John. *Trivia: The Art of Walking the Streets of London.* Forgotten, 2018.
Tolkien, J R R. 'All That Is Gold Does Not Glitter'. *The Lord of the Rings.* Harper Collins, 1995.

Books

Ackroyd, Peter. *London: A Biography.* Vintage, 2001.
Armstrong, Rebecca. *Ovid and His Love Poetry.* Bloomsbury, 2015.
Ballard, J G. *High-Rise.* Jonathan Cape, 1975.
Baudelaire, Charles. *The Painter of Modern Life.* Da Capo, 1964.
Bulson, Eric. *Novels, Maps, Modernity.* Routledge, 2007.
Clare, John. 'First Visit to London', from 'Autobiographical Fragments'. *John Clare by Himself.* John Robinson and David Powell (eds). Carcanet, 2012.
Coverley, Merlin. *Psychogeography.* Harpenden Pocket Essentials, 2006.
Coverley, Merlin. *Occult London.* Oldcastle, 2008.
De Quincey, Thomas. *Confessions of an English Opium Eater.* Penguin, 2003.
Dore, G, & Jerrold, D. *London: A Pilgrimage.* Grant, 1872.
Ford Madox Ford. *The Soul of London.* London, 1905.
Harding, Vanessa. *People in Place.* University of London Press, 2006.
Hill, Rosemary. *Stonehenge.* Profile, 2009.
Grumbridge, Andrew, and Vincent Raison. *Today South London, Tomorrow South London.* Unbound, 2018.
Inwood, Stephen. *A History of London.* Macmillan, 1998.
Joyce, James. *Ulysses.* Penguin, 2000.
Kerouac, Jack. *On the Road.* Penguin, 2000.
Machen, Arthur. *The London Adventure.* Village Press, 1974.
Masterman, C (ed.). *The Heart of Empire.* Fisher Unwin, 1901.
Masterman, C. *From the Abyss.* London, 1902.

Michener, James A. *The Drifters*. Random House, 1971.

Mortlock, C B. 'London Pride'. *Inky Blossoms*. McDonald & Evans, 1949.

Nairn, Ian. *Outrage*. Architectural Press, 1956.

Nairn, Ian. *Nairn's London*. Penguin Classics, 2014.

Ovid. *The Art of Love*. Trans. Tom Payne. Vintage, 2002.

Porter, Roy. *London: A Social History*. Penguin, 1994.

Richardson, Tina. *Walking Inside Out: Contemporary British Psychogeography*. Rowman & Littlefield, 2015.

Self, Will. *Psychogeographies*. Bloomsbury, 2007.

Sinclair, Iain. *Lud Heat*. Skylight, 2012.

Sinclair, Iain. *London Orbital*. Penguin, 2003.

Sinclair, Iain. *Suicide Bridge*. Skylight, 2013.

Solnit, Rebecca. *Wanderlust: A History of Walking*. Granta, 2014.

Stevens, George Alexander. *The Adventures of a Speculist: or, A Journey Through London* (vol. I). Hansebooks, 2017.

Sheppard, Francis. *London: A History*. Oxford University Press, 1998.

Tames, Richard. *A Traveller's History of London*. Cassell, 1992.

Woolf, Virginia. *Jacob's Room*. Oxford University Press, 2008.

Articles

Debord, G. 'Introduction to a Critique of Urban Geography'. Trans. Ken Knabb. In *Critical Geographies: A Collection of Readings*. Harald Bauder and Salvatore Engel-Di Mauro (eds). Praxis, 2008, pp. 23–27.

Driver, F, & D Gilbert. 'Heart of Empire? Landscape, Space and Performance in Imperial London'. *Environment and Planning D: Society and Space 16*(1). Royal Holloway, 1998.

Parrinder, P. 'Heart of Darkness: Geography as Apocalypse'. In *Fears and Fantasies of the Late Nineteenth Century*. J Stokes (ed.). Macmillan, 1992.

Poe, Edgar Allan. 'The Man of the Crowd'. *Burton's Magazine*. London, 1840.

TV & Film

Wood, Michael. *Ovid: The Poet and the Emperor*. Maya Vision for BBC, 2017.

Children of the Revolution (The Urchins' Parade)

Image

'Eros', Piccadilly Circus. Copyright: the author.

Epigraph

Albert Gilbert's comments on his 'Eros' monument in Piccadilly Circus.

Poems

Blake, William. 'Holy Thursday'. *Songs of Innocence and Experience.* Taurus, 1971.
Blake, William. *London.* Taurus, 1976.
Larkin, Philip. 'Deceptions'. *Collected Poems.* Faber & Faber, 2003.
Oxley, William. 'The Bitter Cry of Outcast London'. In *London in Poetry and Prose.* Anna Adams (ed.). Enitharmon, 2002.
Tagore, Rabindranath. 'Poorest, Lowliest, and Lost'. *Gitanjali.* Simon & Schuster, 1997.

Books

Hammond J L, & Barbara Hammond. *Lord Shaftesbury.* Pelican, 1939.
Mayhew, Henry. *London Labour and the London Poor* (vols 2 & 3). Wordsworth, 2008.
Porter, Roy. *London: A Social History.* Penguin, 2000.

Articles

Hetherington, Henry. 'The Factory Girl'. *Destructive.* London, April 1833.

A Vast Unfinished Universe

Image

Westminster Abbey. Copyright: the author.

Epigraph

Dryden, John. 'Mac Flecknoe'. *Complete Works.* Delphi, 2013.

Poems

Anonymous. 'Westminster Abbey; For William Lawrence, D. 1621'. *Oxford Book of Local Verses.* John Holloway (ed.). Oxford University Press, 1987.
Bastard, Thomas. 'Epigram 4:32'. *Chrestoleros.* Manchester, 1888.
Beaumont, Francis. 'On the Tombs in Westminster Abbey'. In *London: A History in Verse.* Mark Ford (ed.). Harvard University Press, 2012.
Betjeman, John. 'In Westminster Abbey'. *Collected Poems.* Murray, 2006.
Betjeman, John. 'The Heart of Thomas Hardy'. *Collected Poems.* Murray, 2006.
Brown, Thomas. 'Westminster Abbey'. *Works of Mr Thomas Brown* (vol. III). London, 1720.
Cope, Wendy. 'Engineers' Corner'. *Making Cocoa for Kingsley Amis.* Faber & Faber, 2010.

Dart, Rev. John. 'Westminster Abbey'. In 'Spenser and the Tradition: English Poetry 1579–1830'. Accessed online May 2018: spenserians.cath.vt.edu

Graves, Robert. 'A Country Mansion'. *Collected Poems*. Cassell, 1991.

Gray, Thomas. 'Elegy Written in a Country Churchyard'. *Thomas Gray: Selected Poems*. Bloomsbury, 1997.

Hardy, Thomas. 'A Refusal'. In *London: A History in Verse*. Mark Ford (ed.). Harvard University Press, 2012.

Hardy, Thomas. 'The Coronation'. In *London: A History in Verse*. Mark Ford (ed.). Harvard University Press, 2012.

Hunt, Leigh. 'Written in Poets' Corner, Westminster Abbey'. In 'Spenser and the Tradition: English Poetry 1579–1830'. Accessed online May 2018: spenserians.cath.vt.edu

Lewis, Alun. 'Westminster Abbey'. In *London: A History in Verse*. Mark Ford (ed.). Harvard University Press, 2012.

Maurice, Rev. Thomas. 'Westminster Abbey: An Elegiac Poem'. In 'Spenser and the Tradition: English Poetry 1579–1830'. Accessed online May 2018: spenserians.cath.vt.edu

May, Winifred Emma (Patience Strong). 'The Sleeping Stone'. Accessed online May 2018: poemhunter.com/poem/the-sleeping-stone

Pope, Alexander. 'Epitaph for One Who Would Not Be Buried in Westminster Abbey'. *Oxford Book of Local Verses*. John Holloway (ed.). Oxford University Press, 1987.

Shirley, James. 'The Last Conqueror'. In *Palgrave's Golden Treasury*. Francis Turner Palgrave and John Press (eds). Oxford University Press, 2002.

Southey, Robert. 'The Alderman's Funeral'. In 'Spenser and the Tradition: English Poetry 1579–1830'. Accessed online May 2018: spenserians.cath.vt.edu

Spurgeon. Charles, W (ed.). *The Poetry of Westminster Abbey*. Including the poems of Thomas Bailey Aldrich, Tom Brown, Aubrey de Vere, Henry Ellison, Sumner Lincoln Fairfield, Owen Howell, Edward Jerningham, Alexander Kay, Joaquin Miller, Thomas Miller, Robert Montgomery, Frederick W H Myers, James Thomson, William Thompson, William Shepperley, George Alexander Stevens, Thomas Tod Stoddart. Xlibris. 2008.

Tennyson, Alfred (Lord). 'Sir John Franklin: On the Cenotaph in Westminster Abbey'. *Oxford Book of Local Verses*. John Holloway (ed.). Oxford University Press, 1987.

Wesley, Samuel Jr. 'The Monument'. *John Wesley Poetry and Hymns, Arminian* (vol. 11). London, 1788.

Yeats, W. B. 'He Wishes for the Cloths of Heaven'. *Collected Poems*. Wordsworth, 2000.

Books

Arnold, Ralph. *The Unhappy Countess*. Constable, 1957.

Dickens, Charles. *The Uncommercial Traveller*. London, 1859.

Dickens, Charles. *The Old Curiosity Shop*. Penguin, 2001.

Dickens, Charles. *Dombey and Son*. Penguin, 2004.

Evelyn, John. *Fumifugium*. London, 1661.

Jenkyns, Richard. *Westminster Abbey: A Thousand Years of National Pageantry*. Profile, 2011.

Joyce, James. *Finnegans Wake*. Oxford University Press, 2012.

Lindsay, Philip. *On Some Bones in Westminster Abbey: A Defence of King Richard III*. Cedric Chivers, 1934.

Moore, Wendy. *Wedlock: The True Story of the Disastrous Marriage and Remarkable Divorce of Mary Eleanor Bowes, Countess of Strathmore*. Three Rivers, 2009.

Nairn, Ian. 'The Abbey'. *Nairn's London*. Penguin, 2014.

Prendergast, Thomas A. *Poetical Dust: Poets' Corner and the Making of Britain*. University of Pennsylvania Press, 2015.

Stoker, Bram. *Dracula*. Penguin, 2004.

Taylor, John. *The Old, Old, Very Old Man, or the Age and Long Life of Thomas Parr* (pamphlet). London, 1635.

Wesley, John. *The Journal of John Wesley*. CreateSpace, 2013.

Willoughby, Tony. *Westminster Abbey and the Navy*. Paragon, 2019.

Articles

'Sir Cloudesley Shovel Shipwrecked'. *History Today*, October 2007, p. 61.

Music and Song

Famous Myers Jubilee Singers. 'Dem Bones'. *Black Vocal Groups, Vol. 4: 1927–1939*. Document, 1997.

What I Did (Obsessive Killing Disorder)

Image

Barriers and deterrents on Hungerford Bridge. Copyright: the author.

Poems

Adams, Anna. 'Crossing Hungerford Bridge'. In *London in Poetry and Prose*. Anna Adams (ed.). Enitharmon, 2002.

Booker, Malika. 'Hungerford Bridge'. *Breadfruit*. Flipped Eye, 2007.

Cope, Wendy. 'After the Lunch'. In *London: A History in Verse*. Mark Ford (ed.). Harvard University Press, 2012.

Eliot, T S. *The Waste Land.* Faber & Faber, 2002.

Fanthorpe, U A. 'Counting Song'. In *London in Poetry and Prose.* Anna Adams (ed.). Enitharmon, 2002.

Hood, Thomas. 'Bridge of Sighs'. *Complete Poetical Works.* BiblioLife, 2009.

Hulme, T. E. 'The Embankment'. In *London: A History in Verse.* Mark Ford (ed.). Harvard University Press, 2012.

Kipling, Rudyard. 'The River's Tale'. In *London: A History in Verse.* Mark Ford (ed.). Harvard University Press, 2012.

Morton, Valerie. 'Hungerford Bridge'. Accessed online May 2018: maryevans.com/poetryblog.php?post_id=7592

Thomas, Dylan. 'A Refusal to Mourn the Death by Fire of a Child in London'. *Collected Poems: Dylan Thomas.* W&N, 2003.

Thomson, James. 'The City of Dreadful Night'. *The City of Dreadful Night.* Book Jungle, 2009.

Walcott, Derek. 'Omeros'. In *London: A History in Verse.* Mark Ford (ed.). Harvard University Press, 2012.

Wilde, Oscar. 'Symphony in Yellow'. *Oscar Wilde, Complete Collection.* CreateSpace, 2014.

Wordsworth, William. 'Upon Westminster Bridge'. In *London: A History in Verse.* Mark Ford (ed.). Harvard University Press, 2012.

Wybrow, Angela. 'View from a Bridge'. Accessed online May 2018: poemhunter.com/poem/view-from-a-bridge

Books

Joyce, James, *Ulysses.* Penguin, 1992.

Koven, S. *Slumming: Sexual and Social Politics in Victorian London.* Princeton, 2004.

London, Jack. *People of the Abyss.* Forgotten Books, 2018.

Orwell, George. *As I Please, 1943–1945: The Collected Essays, Journalism & Letters.* David R Godine, 2000.

Orwell, George. *Down and Out in Paris and London.* Penguin, 2013.

Articles

Lordan, Robert. 'The Devil's Disciple'. *Taxi Magazine*, 9 February 2016, p. 33.

Online

Campbell, Katie. 'Hungerford Bridge'. From St Andrew the Apostle Greek Orthodox School newsletter, October 2017. Accessed online May 2018: standrewtheapostle.org.uk/documents/newsletters/Newsletter_2_-_Oct_2017.pdf

Artworks

Claus, Emile. *Hungerford Bridge*. 1916. Private collection.

Derain, Andre. *Hungerford Bridge at Charing Cross*. 1906. National Gallery of Art, Washington, DC.

Monet, Claude. *Charing Cross Bridge*. 1900. Museum of Art, Indianapolis.

Pissaro, Camille. *Charing Cross Bridge*. 1890. National Gallery of Art, Washington, DC.

Sisley, Alfred. *Charing Cross Bridge*. 1874. National Gallery, London.

Whistler, James. *Charing Cross Bridge*. 1896. Carnegie Museum of Art. Pittsburgh.

Whistler, James. *Old Hungerford Bridge*. 1861. Freer Gallery, Washington, DC.

Music and Song

Coward, Noel. 'London Pride'. *His HMV Recordings 1928–53*. EMI, 1993.

McManus, Declan (Elvis Costello and the Attractions). 'London's Brilliant Parade'. *Brutal Youth*. Warner Bros, 1994.

Traditional. 'Sammy Soapsuds'. In *Nursery Rhymes of England*. James Orchard Halliwell-Phillipps (ed.). London, 1846.

Big Daves Gusset

Image

Warehouse in Borough (now demolished). Copyright: the author.

Poems

Aldington, Richard. 'St Mary's Kensington'. In *London: A History in Verse*. Mark Ford (ed.). Harvard University Press, 2012.

Henson, Stuart. 'Late Train'. In *London in Poetry and Prose*. Anna Adams (ed.). Enitharmon, 2002.

Owen, Wilfred. 'Futility'. *Complete Poems*. Blackthorn, 2013.

Sandburg, Carl. 'Grass'. *Complete Poems*. Houghton Mifflin Harcourt, 2003.

Sandburg, Carl. 'Window'. *Complete Poems*. Houghton Mifflin Harcourt, 2003.

Webster, J. 'A Land Dirge'. In *Palgrave's Golden Treasury*. Francis Turner Palgrave and John Press (eds). Oxford University Press, 2002.

Whitman, Walt. 'To A Common Prostitute'. *Complete Poems of Walt Whitman*. Wordsworth, 1995.

It Tolls for Thee

Image

St Sepulchre church. Copyright: the author.

Epigraph

More, Hannah. 'The Gin Shop'. In *London: A History in Verse*. Mark Ford (ed.). Harvard University Press, 2012.

Poems

Betjeman, John. 'Great Central Railway Sheffield Victoria to Banbury'. *Collected Poems*. Murray, 2006.

Betjeman, John. 'Monody on the Death of Aldersgate Street Station'. *Collected Poems*. Murray, 2006.

Donne, John. 'Meditation 17'. *Complete Poetry and Selected Prose*. Modern Library, 2001.

Gay, John. 'Trivia'. *Walking the Streets by Day*. London, 1716.

Heaney, Seamus. 'District and Circle'. In *London: A History in Verse*. Mark Ford (ed.). Harvard University Press, 2012.

Henley, William Ernest. 'Invictus'. *Book of Verses, Life and Death (Echoes)* (vol. I). London, 1888.

Jonson, Ben. 'On the Famous Voyage'. *Complete Poems*. Penguin, 1988.

Keats, John. 'Lines on the Mermaid Tavern'. In *London: A History in Verse*. Mark Ford (ed.). Harvard University Press, 2012.

Milliken, Edwin J. 'Who is in Charge of the Clattering Train?' *Finest Hour 131*, 2006, p. 28.

Swift, Jonathan. 'Description of a City Shower'. In *London: A History in Verse*. Mark Ford (ed.). Harvard University Press, 2012.

Books

Ackroyd, Peter. *London: The Biography*. Vintage, 2001.

The Bible. King James Version. Oxford University Press, 1998. Matthew 16:26.

Brown, Thomas. *Tom Brown Arrested by the Devil, or, A True and Wonderful Relation How the Devil Met Him on Ludgate Hill*. London, 1698.

Cunningham, Ian. *Writer's London*. Prion, 2001.

Dickens, Charles. *Oliver Twist*. Penguin, 2012.

Dickens, Charles. *Barnaby Rudge*. CreateSpace, 2015.

Dickens, Charles. *Pickwick Papers*. CreateSpace, 2016.

Joyce, James. *Ulysses*. Penguin, 2000.

Mackay, Charles. *Extraordinary Popular Delusions and the Madness of Crowds*. Random House, 2001.

Wilde, Oscar. *The Picture of Dorian Gray*. Penguin, 2003.

Music and Song

Traditional. 'Oranges and Lemons'. In *Nursery Rhymes of England*. James Orchard Halliwell-Phillipps (ed.). London, 1846.

Seat of the Beast

Image

Smithfield Market. Courtesy: Matthew van Gessel.

Poems

Hood, Thomas. 'Ode to the Advocates for the Removal of Smithfield Market'. *Complete Poetical Works*. BiblioLife, 2009.
Hood, Thomas. 'Workhouse Clock'. *Complete Poetical Works*. BiblioLife, 2009.
Patmore, Coventry. 'A London Fête'. In *London: A History in Verse*. Mark Ford (ed.). Harvard University Press, 2012.
Stevens, George Alexander. 'Verse for Bartholomew Fair'. *Oxford Book of Local Verses*. John Holloway (ed.). Oxford University Press, 1987.
Townsend Warner, Sylvia. 'Song from the Bride of Smithfield'. In *London: A History in Verse*. Mark Ford (ed.). Harvard University Press, 2012.
Traditional. 'Jack Sprat'. *Types of Children's Literature*. W Barnes (ed.). New York, 1920.
Wordsworth, William. 'Farmer of Tilsbury Vale'. In *London: A History in Verse*. Mark Ford (ed.). Harvard University Press, 2012.

Books

Dickens, Charles. *Little Dorrit*. Penguin, 2012.
Dickens, Charles. *Oliver Twist*. Penguin, 2012.
Dickens, Charles. *Barnaby Rudge*. CreateSpace, 2015.
Dickens, Charles. *Pickwick Papers*. CreateSpace, 2016.
Doyle, Arthur Conan. 'A Study in Scarlet'. *Complete Sherlock Holmes*. Penguin, 1981.
Haining, Peter. *Sweeney Todd*. Robson, 1993.
Jonson, Ben. *Bartholomew Fair*. Digireads.com, 2011.
Shakespeare, William. *Henry IV, Part 2*. *Complete Works*. Stanley Taylor and Gary Wells (eds). Oxford University Press, 2005.
Stow, John. 'William Fitzstephen's Description of London'. *A Survey of London*. Sutton, 2005.
Velten, Hannah. *Beastly London*. Reaktion, 2013.

Artworks

Bacon, Francis. *Three Studies for Figures at the Base of a Crucifixion*. 1944. Tate Britain, London.
Egg, Augustus Leopold. *Past and Present, No. 3*. 1858. Tate Britain, London.
Hogarth, William. *Roast Beef of Old England*. 1748. Tate Britain, London.

Music

Sondheim, Steven. *Sweeney Todd* (original recording). RCA Red Seal, 1979.

The Italian Boy

Image

St Bartholomew's hospital. Copyright: the author.

Poems

Southey, Robert. 'The Surgeon's Warning'. *Poems* (vol. 2). Gale ECCO, 2012.
Traditional. 'When Adam Delved'.

Books

Blake, William. *An Island in the Moon*. Dodo, 2009.
Moore, Wendy. *The Knifeman*. Broadway, 2006.
Zucchi, John E. 'The Organ Boys in London'. *The Little Slaves of the Harp*. McGill-Queen's, 1998.

Witness Accounts

Old Bailey Online. Witness testimonies of Richard Partridge, Augustine Broom, Joseph Paragelli, Mary Paragelli, Andrew Coller, Martha King, Thomas Mills, John Kirkman, Joseph Higgins. *The Crown v. John Bishop, James May and Thomas Williams, Old Bailey, London, December 2–3, 1831* Accessed online May 2018:
oldbaileyonline.org/browse.jsp?div=t18311201-17

The Truth Is Somewhat More Prosaic

Image

Sarah Smith tiles from Wall of Sacrifice. Copyright: the author.

Books

Darby, Nell. *Life on the Victorian Stage: Theatrical Gossip*. Pen & Sword, 2017.

Articles

Daily News. 'Disaster at the Princess Theatre'. 2 February 1863.
The Era. Letter from William Harris. 1 February 1863.

Films

Nichols, Mike (dir). *Closer*. Columbia, 2004.

Foster Father

Poems

Alighieri, Dante. *Inferno. Divine Comedy*. Penguin, 2003.
Betjeman, John. 'City'. *Collected Poems*. Murray, 2006.
Betjeman, John. 'Diary of a Church Mouse'. *Collected Poems*. Murray, 2006.
Betjeman, John. 'Lines to Martyn Skinner . . .' *Collected Poems*. Murray, 2006.
Betjeman, John. 'Saint Mary Woolnoth'. *Collected Poems*. Murray, 2006.
Larkin, Philip. 'Church Going'. *Collected Poems*. Faber & Faber, 2003.

Books

Russell, John Malcolm. *The Writing on the Wall*. Eisenbrauns, 1999.
Shakespeare, William. *Henry V. Complete Works*. Oxford University Press, 2005.
Mortlock, C B. *Famous London Churches*. Skeffington, 1934.

Articles

Zammit, Abigail. 'Visiting Azekah, Lachish and J L Starkey's resting place'. Palestine Exploration Fund Blog, 1 July 2015. Accessed online May 2018: pef.org.uk/blog/visiting-azekah-lachish-and-j-l-starkeys-resting-place

Last of the Mohicans *(Mio Platano Amato)*

Image

Wood Street plane tree. Copyright: the author.

Epigraph

Woodland Trust description of a London plane tree. Accessed online May 2018: woodlandtrust.org.uk/trees-woods-and-wildlife/british-trees/a-z-of-british-trees/london-plane

Poems

Aldington, Richard. 'St Mary's Kensington'. In *London: A History in Verse*. Mark Ford (ed.). Harvard University Press, 2012.

Cavendish, Margaret. 'A Description of Civil-Warrs'. London, 1656.

Clare, John. 'The Fallen Elm'. *Major Works*. Oxford University Press, 2008.

Clarke, John Cooper. 'Lungs of the World'. Accessed online May 2018: johncooperclarke.com/poems/lungs-of-the-world

Hardy, Thomas. 'To a Tree in London'. *Collected Poems*. Macmillan, 1965.

Hood, Thomas. 'I Remember, I Remember'. *Complete Poetical Works*. BiblioLife, 2009.

Wordsworth, William. 'The Reverie of Poor Susan'. *Best Short Poems*. Shamrock Eden, 2011.

Books

Bucholz, Robert O, & Joseph P Ward. *London: A Social and Cultural History, 1550–1750*. Cambridge University Press, 2012.

Dickens, Charles. *Great Expectations*. London, 1861.

Evelyn, John. *Fumifugium*. London, 1661.

Frazer, James George. *The Golden Bough*. Macmillan, 1890.

Hunt, Leigh. 'The Trees in the City'. *The Town*. London, 1848.

Spraggon, Julie. *Puritan Iconoclasm in the English Civil War*. Boydell, 2003.

Thornbury, Walter. 'Cheapside: Introduction'. *Old and New London: Volume 1*. London, 1878, pp. 304–315.

Time Out Guides. *The Great Trees of London*. Time Out, 2010.

Wells, H G. *Tono Bungay*. Penguin, 2005.

Articles

City of London government. '4.3.4 Heritage Trees: The Cheapside Plane'. Accessed online May 2018: cityoflondon.gov.uk/services/environment-and-planning/planning/heritage-and-design/Documents/Tree-Strategy-Part-2.4-Trees-and-the-Environment-Research.pdf

Clow, Don. 'From Macadam to Asphalt' (part 1). Accessed online May 2018: glias.org.uk/journals/8-a.html

Music and Song

Bennard, George. 'The Old Rugged Cross'. 1912.
Handel, George Frideric. 'Ombra Mai Fu'. In *Xerxes*. Andreas Scholl (artist). Akademie für Alte Musik Berlin (orchestra). Harmonia Mundi, 1999.

Here Lies ...

Image

St Pancras Old Church. Author, from historic image.

Poems

Carroll, Lewis. *The Walrus and the Carpenter*. Boyd Mills, 1998.
Clarke, Jeremy. 'Praise'. *Spatiamentum*. Rufus, 2014
Hardy, Thomas. 'The Levelled Churchyard'. *Collected Poems*. Macmillan, 1965.
Kipling, Rudyard. 'Glory of the Garden'. *Collected Poems*. Wordsworth, 1994.
Nelson, Esther. 'Old King Death'. *Island Minstrelsy: Songs from the Isle of Man*. London, 1839.
Tennyson, Alfred (Lord). 'Cleopatra's Needle'. In *London: A History in Verse*. Mark Ford (ed.). Harvard University Press, 2012.

Books

Dickens, Charles. *A Tale of Two Cities*. London, 1859.
Emery, Philip A, and Kevin Wooldridge. *St Pancras Burial Ground*. Gifford, 2011.
Porter, Roy. *London: A Social History*. Penguin, 2000.

Artworks

Poussin, Nicolas. *Et In Arcadia Ego*. 1638. Louvre, Paris.
Unknown artist. *St Pancras Church and the Adam and Eve Tavern* (early nineteenth century). Camden Local Studies and Archives Centre.

Eden

Image

Kenwood House. Brett Jordan. Free licence from unsplash.com.

Poems

Allott, Kenneth. 'Memento Mori'. In *London: A History in Verse*. Mark Ford (ed.). Harvard University Press, 2012.

Auden, W H. Verse script for *The Londoners*. John Taylor (dir.). Realist Film Unit, 1939.

The Bible. King James Version. Oxford University Press, 1998.

Hunt, Leigh. 'To Hampstead'. In *London: A History in Verse*. Mark Ford (ed.). Harvard University Press, 2012.

Keats, John. 'To One Who Has Been Long in City Pent'. In *London: A History in Verse*. Mark Ford (ed.). Harvard University Press, 2012.

Smith, James, & Horace Smith. 'Ode XV'. *Horace in London*. In *London: A History in Verse*. Mark Ford (ed.). Harvard University Press, 2012.

Spender, Stephen. 'Hampstead Autumn'. In *London: A History in Verse*. Mark Ford (ed.). Harvard University Press, 2012.

Thomson, James. 'Sunday at Hampstead'. In *London: A History in Verse*. Mark Ford (ed.). Harvard University Press, 2012.

Articles

Parker, Emily. 'Second Nature'. *English Heritage Magazine*, May 2018, pp. 36–39.

Artworks

Brown, Ford Madox. *English Autumn Afternoon*. 1853. Birmingham Art Gallery.

Gainsborough, Thomas. *Portrait of John Joseph Merlin*. 1781. Kenwood House, London.

ROMANCING THE BRITISH MUSEUM

Images

Taken at the British Museum by the author.

Poems

Anon. 'Epic of Gilgamesh'. Sumaya Shabandar (trans.). Garnet, 1994.

Aldington, Richard. 'At the British Museum'. 1929. Accessed online May 2018: famouspoetsandpoems.com/poets/richard_aldington/poems/4352

Byron, George Gordon (Lord). 'Childe Harold's Pilgrimage'. 1812–18. Accessed online May 2018: gutenberg.org/files/5131/5131-h/5131-h.htm

Byron, George Gordon (Lord). 'English Bards and Scotch Reviewers'. 1809. Accessed online May 2018: ebooks.adelaide.edu.au/b/byron/george/english-bards-and-scotch-reviewers/the-poem.html

Byron, George Gordon (Lord). 'The Curse of Minerva'. 1811. Accessed online May 2018: hellopoetry.com/poem/4299

Carpenter, Edward. 'Artemidorus, Farewell'. 1896. Accessed online May 2018: poetryexplorer.net/poem.php?id=10046454

Carpenter, Edward. 'In the British Museum Library'. *Towards Democracy*. Taylor & Francis, 2017.

Coleridge, Samuel Taylor. 'Kubla Khan'. 1816. Accessed online May 2018: poetryfoundation.org/poems/43991

Darwin, Erasmus. 'The Botanic Garden'. 1791. Accessed online May 2018: gutenberg.org/cache/epub/9612/pg9612.txt

Donne, John. 'Meditations XVII'. Accessed online May 2018: online-literature.com/donne/409

Doolittle, Hilda. 'The Cliff Temple'. 1916. Accessed online May 2018: poets.org/poetsorg/poem/cliff-temple

Dowden, Edward. 'Antinous Crowned as Bacchus (in the British Museum)'. *Complete Poetry*. Wayne K Chapman (ed.). Liverpool University Press, 2015.

Empson, William. 'Homage to the British Museum'. 1932. Accessed online May 2018: oatridge.co.uk/poems/w/william-empson-homage-to-the-british-museum.php

Frost, Robert. 'The Bad Island – Easter'. 1962. Accessed online May 2018: archive.org/stream/in.ernet.dli.2015.185708/2015.185708.In-The-Clearing-By-Robert-Frost_djvu.txt

Guiney, Louise Imogen. 'In the Reading-Room of the British Museum'. 1893. Accessed online May 2018: poetryfoundation.org/poems/52020/in-the-reading-room-of-the-british-museum

Hardy, Thomas. 'Christmas in the Elgin Room'. In *London in Poetry and Prose*. Anna Adams (ed.). Enitharmon, 2002.

Hardy, Thomas. 'In the British Museum'. In *London in Poetry and Prose*. Anna Adams (ed.). Enitharmon, 2002.

Hamilton, Anne. *Epics of the Ton*. Kessinger, 2010.

Hemans, Felicia. 'Modern Greece'. 1817. Accessed online May 2018: spenserians.cath.vt.edu/TextRecord.php?&action=GET&textsid=36059

Hemans, Felicia. 'The Restoration of the Works of Art to Italy'. London, 1816.

Hunt, Leigh. 'Abou Ben Adhem'. Accessed online May 2018: poetryfoundation.org/poems/44433

Keats, John. 'Ode on a Grecian Urn'. *Complete Poems*. Random House, 1994.

Keats, John. 'Sonnet on the Elgin Marbles'. *Complete Poems*. Random House, 1994.

Keats, John. 'To Haydon on Seeing the Elgin Marbles'. *Complete Poems*. Random House, 1994.

Landor, Walter Savage. 'The Georges'. 1846. Accessed online May 2018: poemhunter.com/poem/the-georges

MacNeice, Louis. 'The British Museum Reading Room'. 1939. Accessed online May 2018: thelondoncolumn.com/2013/07/01/the-british-museum-reading-room

Marvin, Frederic Rowland. 'Cleopatra's Mummy'. *Poems and Translations.* New York, 1907.

Masefield, John. 'The Reading Room'. 1967. Accessed online May 2018: theguardian.com/books/2005/jun/11/featuresreviews.guardianreview11

Maurice, Thomas. 'Hinda; an Eastern Elegy'. 1779. Accessed online May 2018: spenserians.cath.vt.edu/TextRecord.php?action=GET&textsid=39999

Mpanga, George. 'The Benin Bronze'. 2015. Accessed online May 2018: youtube.com/watch?v=3IlUMUGUorw

Nagra, Daljit. 'Meditations on the British Museum'. *British Museum.* Faber & Faber, 2017.

O'Shaughnessy, Arthur. 'Ode'. 1873. Accessed online May 2018: poetryfoundation.org/poems/54933

Plomer, William. 'A Ticket for the Reading Room'. 1940. Accessed online May 2018: thepoeticalcorrectness.blogspot.com/2015/07/william-plomer-1903-1973-charles.html

Pope, Alexander. 'An Essay on Man'. 1732–34. Accessed online May 2018: poetryfoundation.org/poems/44899

Radford, Dollie. 'To the Caryatid (in the Elgin Room)'. 1895. Accessed online May 2018: poemhunter.com/poem/to-the-caryatid

Rossetti, D G. 'The Burden of Nineveh'. 1856, revised 1869. Accessed online May 2018: bartleby.com/270/11/195.html

Shelley, Percy Bysshe. 'England in 1819'. Accessed online May 2018: poetryfoundation.org/poems/45118

Shelley, Percy Bysshe. 'Ozymandias'. 1817. Accessed online May 2018: poemhunter.com/poem/ozymandias

Smith, Horace. 'Ozymandias'. 1817. Accessed online May 2018: poemhunter.com/poem/ozymandias-2

Spraggs, Gillian. 'The Lewis Chessmen'. 1994. Accessed online May 2018: gillianspraggs.com/poems/lewis.html

Tennyson, Alfred (Lord). 'The Two Voices'. 1833. Accessed online May 2018: poemhunter.com/poem/the-two-voices-2

Thomson, Alexander. 'The British Parnassus'. 1801. Accessed online May 2018: spenserians.cath.vt.edu/TextRecord.php?&action=GET&textsid=39249

Wordsworth, William. 'The Egyptian Maid'. 1828. Accessed online May 2018: d.lib.rochester.edu/camelot/text/wordsworth-the-egyptian-maid

Yeats, W B. 'He Wishes for the Cloths of Heaven'. *Collected Poems.* Wordsworth, 2000.

Books

Arkin, Brian. *Builders of My Soul: Greek and Roman Themes in Yeats.* Barnes & Noble, 1991.

Beerbohm, Max. *Enoch Soames.* Hardpress, 2010.

Bernstein, Susan David. *Roomscape: Women Writers in the British Museum.* Edinburgh University Press, 2014.

Boulton, W H. *The Romance of the British Museum.* Sampson Low, Marston, 1934.

Byron, George Gordon (Lord). 'Lord Byron to John Murray, 4 September 1817'. *The Works of Lord Byron* (vol. 1). Aeterna, 2011.

Cayhill, Marjorie L. *The British Museum Reading Room.* British Museum, 2000.

Cheeke, Stephen. *Writing for Art: The Aesthetics of Ekphrasis.* Manchester University Press, 2008.

Curtis, John, and Nigel Tallis (eds). *Forgotten Empire: The World of Ancient Persia.* University of California Press, 2005.

De Volney, C F. *Ruins of Empires.* New York, 1851.

Dickens, Charles. 'Shabby-Genteel People'. *Sketches by Boz.* Penguin, 1996.

Gidal, Eric. *Poetic Exhibitions: Romantic Aesthetics and the Pleasures of the British Museum.* Bucknell University Press, 2002.

Gissing, George. *New Grub Street.* Oxford University Press, 2009.

Hawthorne, Deanna Fernie. *Sculpture, and the Question of American Art.* Routledge, 2011.

Hebron, Stephen. *The Romantics and the British Landscape.* British Library, 2006.

Jenkins, Ian. *Archaeologists and Aesthetes in the Sculpture Galleries of the British Museum 1800–1939.* British Museum, 1992.

Jenkins, Tiffany. *Keeping Their Marbles: How the Treasures of the Past Ended Up in Museums.* British Museum, 2018.

Larrabee, Stephen. *English Bards and the Grecian Marbles.* Forgotten, 2018.

Lodge, David. *The British Museum Is Falling Down.* Vintage, 2011.

Lowes, John Livingston. *The Road to Xanadu.* Princeton University Press, 2016.

Maurice, Thomas. *Indian Antiquities.* Gale Ecco, 2010.

Maurice, Thomas. *The History of Hindostan.* London, 1795–98.

Rood, Tim. 'Horoscopes of Empires: Future Ruins from Thucydides to Macaulay'. In *Knowing Future Time Through Greek Historiography.* Alexandra Lianeri (ed.). De Gruyter, 2016.

Woolf, Virginia. *Jacob's Room.* Oxford University Press, 2008.

Woolf, Virginia. *A Room of One's Own.* Stronck, 2013.

Yeats, W B. *The Trembling of the Veil.* BiblioLife, 2009.

Articles

Pound, Ezra. 'A Few Don'ts by an Imagiste'. *Poetry Magazine*, March 1913.

Molloy, Frank. 'British Museum Gets Lyrical'. British Museum Blog, 28 September 2017. Accessed online May 2018: blog.britishmuseum.org /poetic-licence-the-museum-gets-lyrical

Rodenbeck, John. 'Travelers from an Antique Land: Shelley's Inspiration for Ozymandias'. *Alif: Journal of Comparative Poetics 24,* 2004, pp. 121–148.

Music

Gershwin, Ira, & George Gershwin. 'A Foggy Day (in London Town)'. 1937.

GHOSTS OF SWINGING LONDON

Images

Copyright: the author.

Books

Blake, Mark. *Pink Floyd: Pigs Might Fly.* Aurum, 2013.

Davies, Hunter. *The Beatles.* Ebury, 2009.

Hewitt, Paolo. *Small Faces: The Young Mods' Forgotten Story.* Acid Jazz, 2010.

Jagger, Mick. *According to the Rolling Stones.* W&N, 2004.

John, Elton. *Me.* Macmillan, 2019.

Jones, Dylan. *David Bowie: A Life.* Windmill, 2018.

Jovanovic, Rob. *God Save the Kinks.* Aurum, 2014.

Leigh, Spencer. *Simon & Garfunkel: Together Alone.* McNidder & Grace, 2015.

Marshall, Ben. *The Who: The Official History.* Virgin, 2015.

Norman, Philip. *Paul McCartney: The Biography.* W&N, 2017.

Richard, Cliff. *My Life My Way.* Headline, 2009.

Shapiro, Harry. *Alexis Korner: The Biography.* Bloomsbury, 1997.

Shelton, Robert. *Bob Dylan: No Direction Home.* Omnibus, 2011.

Stewart, Rod. *Rod: The Autobiography.* Arrow, 2013.

Wall, Mick. *Led Zeppelin: When Giants Walked the Earth.* Orion, 2009.

Online

Baker, Rob. 'Another Nickel in the Machine'. Accessed online May 2018: nickelinthemachine.com

Thanks to Brian Hawkins and Robert Brooks for their recollections on the Marquee and La Chasse.

ROUTES & MAPS

ROUTE FOR SOUL CITY WANDERING

Point 1 ('Children of the Revolution'): Piccadilly Circus

Start at statue of 'Eros' (Anteros), Piccadilly Circus.

Point 2 ('A Vast Unfinished Universe'): Westminster Abbey

Walk down Lower Regent Street and continue southbound via Waterloo Place, Duke of York's Steps, Horse Guards Road and Storey's Gate to Westminster Abbey. Check website beforehand for visiting info.

The route inside, starting from the north aisle, hits these points:

- Scientists' Corner: on the north side of the nave, just before the rood screen.
- Baron Mendip: no dedicated gravestone. A mention of his resting place is in an inscription on the monument to his nephew Charles Agar, Archbishop of Dublin, on the north wall of the north quire aisle, just inside the blue gates.
- Nightingale (Gascoigne) monument: St Michael's chapel in the north transept, parallel to the high altar.
- Lady Elland: white marble gravestone on the floor in the north ambulatory.
- Royal tombs: behind altar and in and around the Lady chapel at the east end.
- Thomas Hardy: beige square stone on the floor in Poets' Corner.
- Thomas Parr: small white oblong stone on the floor of Poets' Corner.
- Mary Eleanor Bowes: well-worn black gravestone on the floor in Poets' Corner. Immediately to the left of the memorial stone to Thomas Parr.
- Robert Hauley: well-worn black gravestone on the floor opposite John Dryden's monument in Poets' Corner.
- Sir Cloudesley Shovell: monument on south quire aisle wall, to right of south-eastern door to cloisters.
- Cosmati pavement: on the floor of the main altar.
- Tomb of the Unknown Soldier: at the western end of the church on the floor, just inside the entrance.

Point 3 ('What I Did'): Hungerford Bridge, Embankment

Cross Parliament Square towards Westminster Bridge and walk along Victoria Embankment to Embankment station, or take the tube from Westminster station one stop to Embankment station. Exit via the south entrance. Climb the stairs on the riverside up to Hungerford Bridge.

Point 4 ('Big Daves Gusset'): Redcross Way, Southwark

Take the stairs adjacent to Hungerford Bridge up to Charing Cross railway station. Take any of the regular trains to London Bridge. Exit via the main entrance and walk down to Borough High Street. Turn left and walk southbound. Turn right onto Southwark Street and left onto Redcross Way. Walk southbound towards the junction with Union Street. Crossbones graveyard tribute is on the left.

Point 5 ('It Tolls for Thee'): City Thameslink Station

Return to London Bridge station and take any of the regular trains to City Thameslink station; get on at the front of the train. Exit via the north entrance and step out onto Newgate Street opposite St Sepulchre Church.

Point 6 ('Seat of the Beast'): Smithfield Market, West Smithfield

Walk down Snow Hill to the left of St Sepulchre Church. Cock Lane is on your right. Turn right onto Smithfield Street and right onto West Smithfield.

Point 7 ('The Italian Boy'): St Bartholomew's Hospital, Giltspur Street

Walk southbound along Giltspur Street.

Point 8 ('The Truth Is Somewhat More Prosaic'): Postman's Park, Aldersgate

Turn left onto Newgate Street and walk eastbound past the bombed-out remains of Christchurch Greyfriars. Turn left onto King Edward Street. Postman's Park is on the right.

Point 9 ('Foster Father'): St Vedast Church, Foster Lane

From Postman's Park turn right onto Aldersgate Street, left onto Gresham St and right onto Foster Lane.

Point 10 ('Last of the Mohicans'): Wood Street Junction with Cheapside

To the left of St Vedast church on Foster Lane, follow the alleyway Priest Court to Gutter Lane. Take Goldsmith Street opposite, then turn right onto Wood St and follow to its junction with Cheapside.

Point 11 ('Here Lies ...'): St Pancras Gardens, Pancras Road

Turn right onto Cheapside and follow westbound to St Paul's Cathedral. From St Paul's steps, walk westbound down Ludgate Hill to City Thameslink station.

Take a train to St Pancras International station. Leave via the western exit (Midland Road). Turn right and walk northbound along Midland Road and Pancras Road. St Pancras Old Church is on your right.

Point 12 ('Eden'): Kenwood House, Hampstead Lane

Return to St Pancras station and take the Northern line underground to Hampstead station. Walk northbound along Heath Street, then take the right fork along Spaniards Road and Hampstead Lane. Follow to Kenwood House.

Afterwards, return to St Pancras station, the nearest major transport hub. With the postscript in mind, you may wish to hail an iconic London black cab to do this.

ROUTE FOR BRITISH MUSEUM

Note: Romancing the British Museum has been structured so that visitors can interact with the exhibits along a logical route. Some room entrances may be closed occasionally. Ask a member of staff for alternative access routes.

Point 1: Great Court

Enter museum via front entrance. Pass through foyer into the Great Court. The inscription from Tennyson's The Two Voices is on the floor near the base of the right-hand staircase around the old Reading Room.

Point 2: Reading Room

The inside can only be accessed by purchasing a ticket for an exhibition held therein. Otherwise, it can only be viewed from the outside.

Point 3: King's Library

Enter the King's Gallery from the Great Court (to the right of the Reading Room). The inscription from Pope's 'Essay on Man' is on the entablature above the south entrance to the King's Gallery.

Point 4: Clytie (Room 1: King's Library)

On entering King's Library from the Great Court, the bust is on the right.

Point 5: Indian Antiquities (Room 1: King's Library)

Indian Antiquities volumes are in the King's Library, in the bookcase on the opposite wall to the entrance from the Great Court (fourth shelf up in case no. 188).

Point 6: Ramesses the Great (Room 4: Egyptian Galleries)

From the King's Library, return to the Great Court and walk to the opposite side of the Reading Room. On entering Room 4, the Rosetta Stone display is facing you. The Ramesses statue is to the right of this display.

Point 7: Mausolus and Artemisia (Room 21: Halicarnassus)

Pass through Room 4 (behind the statue of Ramesses) to the West Stairs landing. Take steps down to the right of the stairwell. Go through the doors and take steps up into Room 21. The statues are facing you.

Point 8: Caryatid (Room 19: Greek Galleries)

From Room 21, go through the entrance to Room 20 (to the right when facing the statues of Mausolus and Artemisia). Pass through into Room 19. As you exit Room 19, the caryatid is on the right.

Point 9: Parthenon Sculptures (Room 18: Duveen Gallery)

From Room 19, go through Room 17 (Nereid monument). Turn right into Room 18 (Duveen Gallery). The Parthenon sculptures adorn the room.

Point 10: Parthenon Sculptures (Room 18: Duveen Gallery)

In the Duveen Gallery (Room 18), the 'Keats lowing heifer' is on the opposite wall on entering Room 18 (south frieze panels 132–136).

Point 11: Assyrian Bulls (Room 10: Assyrian Galleries)

From the Duveen Gallery (Room 18), return to Room 17 and pass through into Room 23. Turn right. Bulls are facing you in Room 10.

Point 12: Antinous as Bacchus (Room 70: Upper Floor)

Pass through Assyrian galleries (Rooms 10, 7 and 6). At the end of Room 6, turn left and pass through the south cloakroom and shop to the main foyer. Turn sharp left and up the South Stairs. At the top of stairs turn sharp right and pass through Rooms 68 and 69 into Room 70. The bust is on a plinth on the right near the centre of the room.

Point 13: Portland Vase (Room 70: Upper Floor)

In Room 70, the vase is in a glass display case on the right in the centre of the room as you go towards Room 71.

Point 14: Mummy of Artemidorus (Room 62: Upper Floor)

Pass through Rooms 71, 72, 73, and upper landing into room 61. Turn right and into Room 62. Mummy is in glass display case on the left in centre of room.

Point 15: Flood Tablet (Room 55: Upper Floor)

From Room 62, pass through into Room 63. Turn right into Room 56. Turn left and pass through into Room 55. The tablet is in a glass display case on the right at the end of the room.

Point 16: Pediment (Exit):

Pass through Room 54 and take East Stairs down to ground level. Turn left and pass through Room 4 (King's Library). Turn right for Great Court and the exit. The pediment is above the main entrance outside.

ROUTE FOR GHOSTS OF SWINGING LONDON

Note: The twelve-stop route takes in ten pubs. All were still operating at the time of writing. If you need to be told to 'drink responsibly', please do not attempt the pub crawl.

Point 1: Denmark Street

Start at Tottenham Court Road tube station. Walk down Charing Cross Road and turn left onto Denmark Street.

Point 2: Moor Street: Spice of Life

From Denmark Street, turn left onto Charing Cross Road. Walk a short distance and turn right onto Moor Street.

Point 3: Great Newport Street: The Porcupine

From Moor Street, turn right onto Charing Cross Road and left onto Litchfield Street. Then return to Charing Cross Road and turn left. After a short distance, turn left onto Great Newport Street.

Point 4: Wardour Street: O'Neill's

From Great Newport Street, cross Charing Cross Rd onto Little Newport Street/Lisle Street. Turn left onto Leicester Place. Return to Lisle Street, turn left, then right onto Wardour Street and walk to junction with Gerrard Street.

Point 5: Macclesfield Street: De Hems

From Wardour Street, turn right onto Gerrard Street. Halfway down Gerrard Street, turn onto Macclesfield Street.

Point 6: Old Compton Street: Compton's

From Macclesfield Street turn right onto Shaftesbury Avenue. Turn left onto Frith Street, then left onto Old Compton Street.

Point 7: Brewer Street: Residence Bar

Turn right onto Wardour Street and walk to junction with Brewer Street.

Point 8: Wardour Street: The Ship

Continue northwards on Wardour Street to junction with Flaxman Court.

Point 9: D'Arblay Street: The George

Follow Flaxman Court around the corner to St Anne's Court. Then turn right onto Wardour Street and walk to the junction with D'Arblay Street.

Point 10: Great Marlborough Street: Coach & Horses

Continue northwards on Wardour Street. Turn left onto Noel Street and walk to junction with Berwick Street. Continue westwards on Noel Street to Great Marlborough Street.

Point 11: Carnaby Street: Shakespeare's Head

Continue westwards on Great Marlborough Street, then turn left onto Carnaby Street. Foubert's Place is off Carnaby Street.

Point 12: Finish

Return to Great Marlborough Street. Turn left, then turn right into Argyll Street. Turn left onto Oxford Street for Oxford Circus tube station.

Map for Soul City Wandering

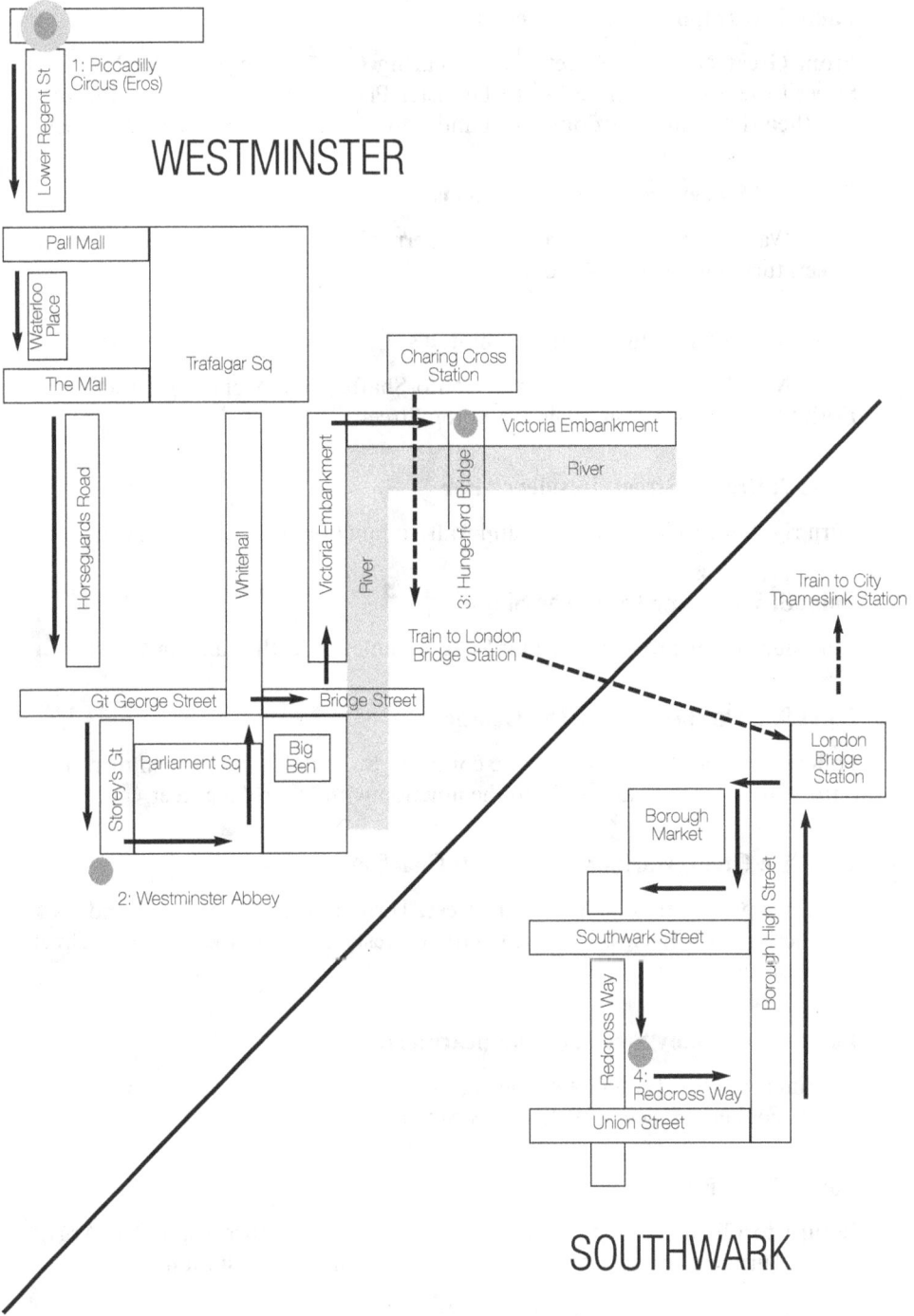

WESTMINSTER

1: Piccadilly Circus (Eros)

Lower Regent St

Pall Mall

Waterloo Place

The Mall

Trafalgar Sq

Horseguards Road

Whitehall

Charing Cross Station

Victoria Embankment

Victoria Embankment

River

3: Hungerford Bridge

River

Gt George Street

Bridge Street

Storey's Gt

Parliament Sq

Big Ben

2: Westminster Abbey

Train to City Thameslink Station

Train to London Bridge Station

London Bridge Station

Borough Market

Borough High Street

Southwark Street

Redcross Way

4: Redcross Way

Union Street

SOUTHWARK

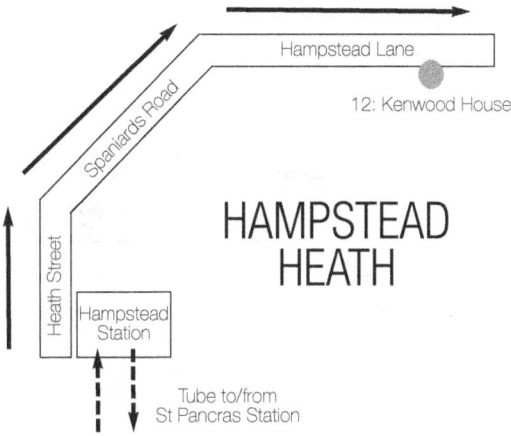

HAMPSTEAD HEATH

Hampstead Lane

12: Kenwood House

Spaniards Road

Heath Street

Hampstead Station

Tube to/from
St Pancras Station

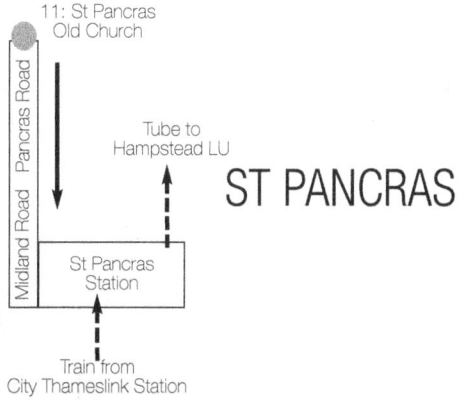

ST PANCRAS

11: St Pancras
Old Church

Pancras Road

Midland Road

Tube to
Hampstead LU

St Pancras
Station

Train from
City Thameslink Station

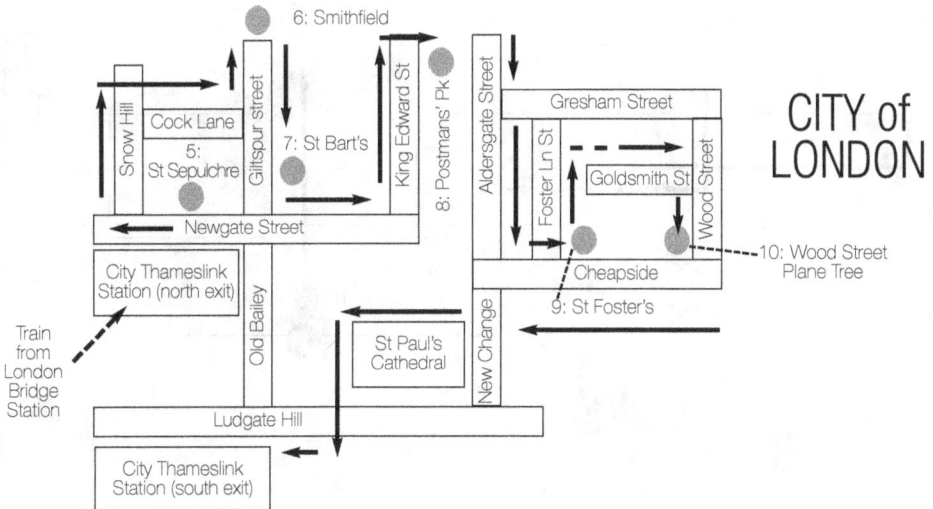

CITY of LONDON

6: Smithfield

Snow Hill

Cock Lane

5: St Sepulchre

Giltspur street

7: St Bart's

King Edward St

8: Postmans' Pk

Aldersgate Street

Gresham Street

Foster Ln St

Goldsmith St

Wood Street

10: Wood Street Plane Tree

Newgate Street

City Thameslink Station (north exit)

Train from London Bridge Station

Old Bailey

St Paul's Cathedral

New Change

Cheapside

9: St Foster's

Ludgate Hill

City Thameslink Station (south exit)

Map for British Museum

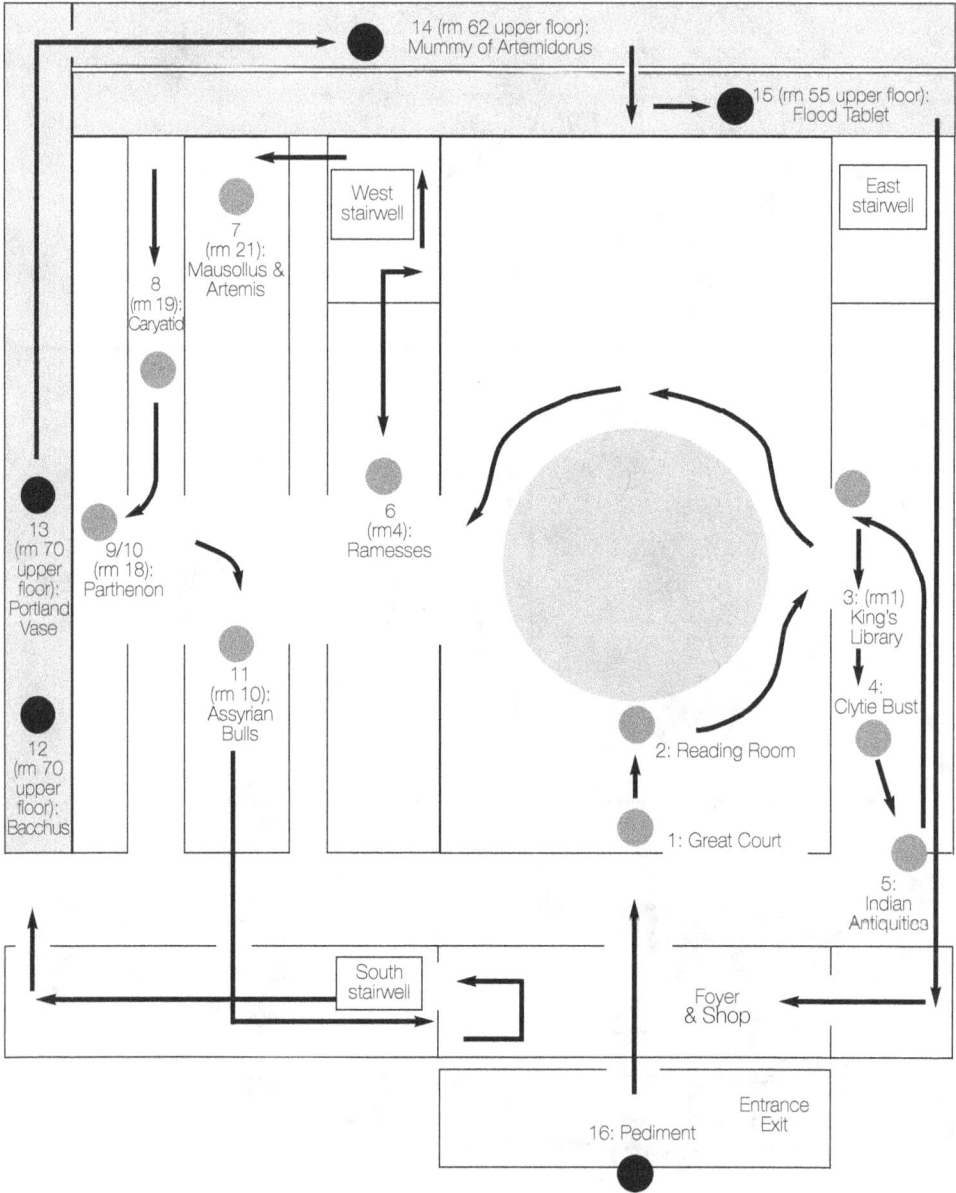

14 (rm 62 upper floor):
Mummy of Artemidorus

15 (rm 55 upper floor):
Flood Tablet

West
stairwell

East
stairwell

7
(rm 21):
Mausollus &
Artemis

8
(rm 19):
Caryatid

6
(rm4):
Ramesses

3: (rm1)
King's
Library

13
(rm 70
upper
floor):
Portland
Vase

9/10
(rm 18):
Parthenon

4:
Clytie Bust

11
(rm 10):
Assyrian
Bulls

2: Reading Room

12
(rm 70
upper
floor):
Bacchus

1: Great Court

5:
Indian
Antiquities

South
stairwell

Foyer
& Shop

Entrance
Exit

16: Pediment

Map for Ghosts of Swinging London

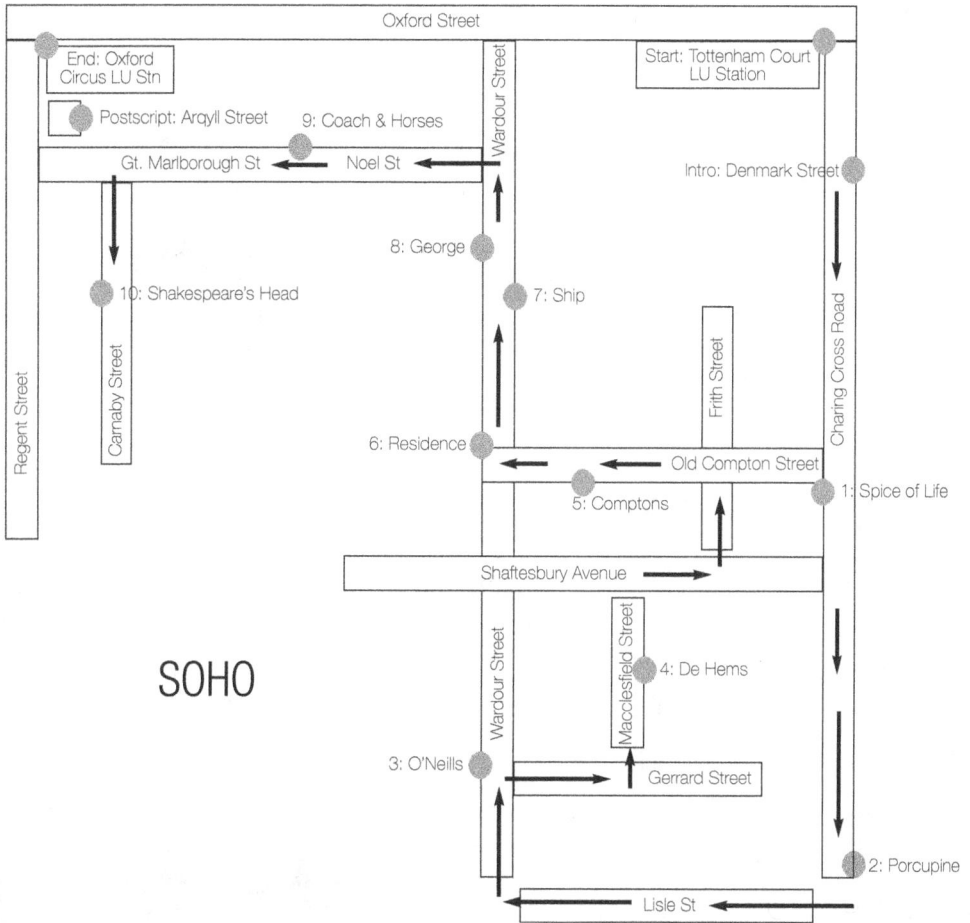

Oxford Street

Wardour Street

End: Oxford Circus LU Stn

Start: Tottenham Court LU Station

Postscript: Argyll Street

9: Coach & Horses

Intro: Denmark Street

Gt. Marlborough St

Noel St

8: George

7: Ship

Charing Cross Road

10: Shakespeare's Head

Regent Street

Carnaby Street

Frith Street

6: Residence

Old Compton Street

1: Spice of Life

5: Comptons

Shaftesbury Avenue

SOHO

Macclesfield Street

4: De Hems

Wardour Street

3: O'Neills

Gerrard Street

2: Porcupine

Lisle St

YOU CAN GO
YOUR OWN WAY

FINDING A THEME

'The streets of London have their map; but our passions are uncharted. What are you going to meet if you turn this corner?'

Virginia Woolf, *Jacob's Room*

Moving with Meaning

Below are some examples and ideas to help you devise your own psychogeographic walks or journeys in London. There are no set rules. Just use some reverie and imagination to encounter places, people or events on your travels.

Pods v. Peds

Experiences are not confined to walking. Iain Sinclair divided schools of psychogeographers into 'peds' (walkers or cyclists) and 'pods' (drivers or public transport users). Any mode of transport can be employed. Whatever floats your boat. Indeed, even boats.

Going Underground

Beneath the pavement, sunk in the earth, hollow drains lined with yellow light forever conveyed them this way and that, and large letters upon enamel plates represented in the underworld the parks, squares, and circuses of the upper.

Virginia Woolf, *Jacob's Room*

Of course, in London, you can utilise the famous tube network for rapid transit between psychogeographic points. For years, revellers have used the system to create themed large-scale pub crawls. Great fun, but at the same time the journeys they are undertaking have an element of the profound. On the London Monopoly board pub crawl, for example, we have a parallel in the value of money: from the word 'Go' you start off sensing the relative poverty of the Old Kent Road and literally follow the wealth all the way to Mayfair. Indeed, the experience conversely hits you in the pocket as your liquid propellant becomes more and more expensive along the way! Meanwhile, on the Circle Line pub crawl, it may slowly dawn on you as you try to negotiate the chaotic spirals of London, with the added disorientating effects of alcohol, that the 'Circle' becomes the only constant pattern, your comfort zone and your security blanket. It's a comparable pissed-up version of Sinclair's *London Orbital*.

(Again, if you need to be told to 'drink responsibly', please do not attempt any of the above.)

London's tube system in itself can make for an atmospheric jaunt along its psychological arteries. You can literally submerge yourself in the netherworld of the city, discerning the make-up, disposition and vibes of the temporary troglodytes as they wait on platforms on Saturday evenings or Monday mornings.

Think Dimensionally

Look up! Modern cities have generated an expansive new plateau to explore, with sky gardens, rooftop restaurants and viewing platforms. If little else, it may give you a different perspective on life.

Psycho-Pops

Experiences don't necessarily have to involve high levels of esotericism. If you wish, take a 'psy-geo-lite' approach and focus on the mainstream. For an example, see *Ghosts of Swinging London*. This is a crawl around the Soho pubs once frequented by rock 'n' roll legends of the sixties, unearthing the lost music venues, and listening to a fitting soundtrack along the way.

Going just a little deeper, you could explore London's pockets of soul as a theme. For example, if you work in the City of London, where the soul is easy to buy, you might seek out the antidote to the unforgiving hustle and bustle. It might be the ghostly bombed-out remains of Christchurch Greyfriars, the poignant Wall of Sacrifice in Postman's Park, or the rugged old plane tree on the corner of Wood Street. You could do this over a period of time and put it to practical use, such as searching out tranquil sanctuaries for lunch breaks.

Pilgrim's Progress

Recreate a psychogeographic journey of the past, perhaps of a figure you find inspirational. It might help you to interpret their influence on you. This, in effect, is a kind of homage.

In 2000, Iain Sinclair retraced the footsteps of the poet John Clare, who absconded from an asylum in 1841. The epic eighty-mile journey from Epping Forest to Northborough in Cambridgeshire helped Sinclair forge his own personal bond with Clare.

Salute Your Commute

Don't look on your journey to work as dull. Celebrate it. Look for anything that could help you take back control of your environment. Can you play with street names? Can you forge an interpretation of colours? Can you recognise serendipity with numbers? Sinclair made great comic use of reciting examples of the inane emptiness of modern advertising blurbs on a regular journey he took.

I plugged into the blue plaque luminaries that I pass on my usual drive through suburban London. Reading like a dream team of creative emotion, they are, in order, Sir Arthur Conan Doyle, Emile Zola, Raymond Chandler, Sax Rohmer, John Ruskin, Dan Leno, Vincent van Gogh and William Blake.

You might ask where the reciprocal psychological factor is: how do these environmental points affect me? Well, they are all on the shortcuts and rat-runs that I take to avoid raging at rush-hour traffic like a lunatic. On my course through Norwood, Brixton and Lambeth, and up to the Thames, the guiding lights on my personal ley line keep me sane . . . before I cross the river . . . and the great vistas of *my city* glide and muscle into view.

www.ingramcontent.com/pod-product-compliance
Lightning Source LLC
Chambersburg PA
CBHW060845280326
41934CB00007B/926